John Harcourt

Directory of St. Paul's Reformed Episcopal Church of Chicago

John Harcourt

Directory of St. Paul's Reformed Episcopal Church of Chicago

ISBN/EAN: 9783337296247

Printed in Europe, USA, Canada, Australia, Japan

Cover: Foto ©Lupo / pixelio.de

More available books at **www.hansebooks.com**

THE CHICAGO
Athenæum,

A Society devoted to the welfare of the public, especially of the

Young People of Chicago.

Maintaining for their benefit a

Reading Room, Library, Chess Room, Gymnasium,
Lecture Courses, Sociables, day and evening
Class instruction in Literature, An-
cient and Modern Languages,
Vocal and Instrumental
Music, Elocution,
Phonography,
Drawing, Penmanship, Book-keeping, and the com-
mon and higher English Branches.

All its privileges are furnished at nominal rates to its members,
placing them within the reach of any young man or woman in
the city.

THE ATHENÆUM occupies three entire floors at Nos. 63
and 65 Washington Street, and is now prepared to accommodate a larger membership than ever before.

All persons interested in its work, or desiring to avail themselves of its privileges, are invited to become members.

HENRY BOOTH, *President.*

FERD. W. PECK, *Secretary.*   **O. C. GIBBS,** *Superintendent.*

A BEAUTIFUL

Jewelry Store!

THE PALATIAL JEWELRY STORE OF

N. MATSON & Co.

Cor. State and Monroe Sts.,

is admitted by all who have seen it and are familiar with the business palaces of other cities and other lands, to be, without any exag.
geration, the most elegant store in the world. Its costly marble
counters, its richly carved cases, and its dazzling display of jewelry,
bronzes, silverware, etc., make it, at all times of the year, one of the
most notable sights of Chicago, which no visitor to the city should
miss seeing. There is no other article in purchasing which the buyer
must trust more entirely to the seller's reputation than in the selection of jewelry. Alloys and imitations are so perfect as to deceive
the most expert buyers; but having dealt with this house for years,
we know that they can be implicitly trusted. The greatest ignora-
mus can trade there and be as sure of getting good goods at fair
prices and of being as courteously waited upon as my lady whose
bills foot up $5,000 a year. Their capital is so ample that panics
never cramp them, and their trade is so large that they have the first
choice of the market. This year they have taken advantage of the
dull times to buy largely at prices much lower than ever before, and
for this reason can afford to sell at better prices than any other house
in the city.—*The Advance.*

DIRECTORY

—OF—

ST. PAUL'S

Reformed Episcopal Church,

OF CHICAGO,

CONTAINING

*A brief sketch of the history of the Reformed Episcopal
Church and of St. Paul's Church in particular;
Also a complete list of the present members
alphabetically arranged, together
with a list of the various
organizations connected
with the Church.*

BY

JOHN HARCOURT,

APRIL, 1876.

[FIRST EDITION.]

R. J. KROFF, Publisher,

Room 12 Methodist Church Block,

CHICAGO.

The Appeal.

PREFACE.

This Epitome is designed as an unpretending auxiliary in furtherance of the good work aimed at by Dr. FALLOWS and his worthy coadjutors. In it will be found a truthful history of St. Paul's Reformed Episcopal Church, of Chicago, situated on Washington Street, near Ann Street, together with such general items as I deemed of chief interest.

Its hurried compilation, and the great difficulties to contend with, by reason of the but recent organization of the Church, must be my excuse for any errors that may appear upon its pages. I gratefully acknowledge the assistance rendered me by the Rev. SAMUEL FALLOWS, D. D., and Col. JOHN W. BENNETT, and hope that with the arrival of another year a new directory may be needed, much enlarged and improved, one that will keep pace with the glorious, prosperous future, which, we prayerfully trust, may be in store for St. Paul's Reformed Episcopal Church.

JOHN HARCOURT.

ORGANIZATION

OF THE

REFORMED EPISCOPAL CHURCH.

Taken from the Journal of the First General Council.

On the second of December, 1873, after a meeting of solemn praise and prayer, certain ministers and laymen, formerly connected with the "Protestant Episcopal Church in the United States of America," assembled at ten o'clock A. M., in the building of the Young Men's Christian Association, in the City of New York.

The Right Reverend GEORGE DAVID CUMMINS, D.D., at the close of the devotional exercises, said:

CHRISTIAN BRETHREN: By the goodness of God, and under the protection of the just and equal laws of this Republic, and in the exercise of the invaluable "liberty wherewith Christ hath made us free," you are assembled here to-day in response to the Circular Letter which I will now read:

NEW YORK, *November 13th, 1873.*

DEAR BROTHER,—

The Lord has put into the hearts of some of his servants who are, or have been, in the Protestant Episcopal Church, the purpose of restoring the old paths of their fathers, and of returning to the use of the Prayer Book of 1785, set forth by the General Convention of that year, under the special guidance of the venerable William White, D.D., afterwards the first Bishop of the same church in this country.

JAMES EVANS, Secretary and Treasurer.
H. T. MERRILL, President.   Wm. H. CRAIG, Gen'l Agent.

THE

Apollo Manufacturing Co.,

MANUFACTURERS OF THE

APOLLO ORGAN,

*For Parlors, Drawing Rooms, Libraries, Schools, Lecture
Rooms, Lodges and Churches. Also, the beautiful*

APOLLO PIANO-FORTE

Or Boudoir Piano.

**Pianos and Organs Sold on Monthly and Quarterly Payments,
Also Rented and the money Applied on Purchase.**

*PIANOS AND ORGANS TUNED, REPAIRED AND POL-
ISHED BY EXPERIENCED WORKMEN.*

ALSO

Instruments Moved, Packed and Shipped

TO ANY PART OF THE COUNTRY.

OFFICE:

**No. 8 Methodist Church Block, Chicago, Ill.
Factory: Clinton St., near Randolph.**

N. B.—Every Instrument sold is guarantied to give satisfaction, or the money will be refunded.

The chief features of that Prayer Book, as distinguished from the one now in use, are the following:

1. The word "*Priest*" does not appear in the book, and there is no countenance whatever to the errors of sacerdotalism.

2. The Baptismal Offices, the Confirmation Office, the Catechism, and the Order for the administration of the Lord's Supper, contain no sanction of the errors of Baptismal Regeneration, the Real presence of the Body and Blood of Christ in the elements of the Communion, and of a sacrifice offered by a Priest in that Sacred Feast.

These are the main features that render the Prayer Book of 1785 a thoroughly Scriptural Liturgy, such as all Evangelical Christians who desire Liturgical Worship can use with a good conscience.

On Tuesday, the 2d day of December, 1873, a meeting will be held in Association Hall, corner of Twenty-Third Street and Fourth Avenue, in the City of New York, at 10 o'clock A.M., to organize an Episcopal Church on the basis of the Prayer Book of 1785, a basis broad enough to embrace all who hold "the faith once delivered to the saints," as that faith is maintained by the Reformed Churches of Christendom; with no exclusive and unchurching dogmas toward Christian brethren who differ from them in their views of polity and church order.

This meeting you are cordially and affectionately invited to attend. The purpose of the meeting is to *organize*, and not to discuss the expediency of organizing. A verbatim reprint of the Prayer Book of 1785 is in press, and will be issued during the month of December. May the Lord guide you and us by His Holy Spirit.

GEORGE DAVID CUMMINS.

Bishop Cummins then nominated Col. Benjamin Aycrigg, of New Jersey, as Temporary President; and Mr. William S. Doughty nominated Herbert B. Turner, of New Jersey, as Temporary Secretary.

These officers were duly elected and took their seats.

Bishop Cummins then read a proposed Declaration of Principles, and moved its reference to a Committee of five. Seconded and carried.

The Chair appointed, as such Committee:

Bishop Cummins,
Rev. Marshall B. Smith, of New Jersey,
Dr. G. A. Sabine, of New York,
Mr. Albert Crane, of Illinois, and
Mr. Charles D. Kellogg, of New Jersey.

The meeting then took a recess to await the report of the Committee.

After the expiration of about twenty minutes, the President called the meeting to order, and Bishop Cummins, from the Committee, made the following

T. WICKERSHAM,

Portrait Painter.

First-class Portraits painted in Oil
or Crayon from life. Also
from Photographs, Tintypes,
Ambrotypes or Da-
guerreotypes.

Satisfaction Guaranteed in all Cases.

Room 29 McCormick's Block,

Randolph and Dearborn Streets,

CHICAGO.

☞Take Elevator.

REPORT.

The Committee, appointed to consider the "Declaration of Principles" proposed by Bishop Cummins as the basis of organization of the Reformed Episcopal Church, do now return the same to this meeting, and offer the following resolution:

Resolved, That we whose names are appended to the call for this meeting, as presented by Bishop Cummins, do here and now, in humble reliance upon Almighty God, organize ourselves into a Church, to be known by the style and title of the *"Reformed Episcopal Church,"* in conformity with the following *Declaration of Principles,* and with the Right Reverend George David Cummins, D.D., as our presiding Bishop :

I.

The Reformed Episcopal Church, holding "the faith once delivered unto the saints," declares its belief in the Holy Scriptures of the Old and New Testaments as the Word of God, and the sole Rule of Faith and practice; in the Creed "commonly called the Apostles' Creed;" in the Divine institution of the Sacraments of Baptism and the Lord's Supper; and in the doctrines of grace substantially as they are set forth in the thirty-nine articles of religion.

II.

This Church recognizes and adheres to Episcopacy, not as of divine right, but as a very ancient and desirable form of church polity.

III.

This Church retaining a Liturgy which shall not be imperative or repressive of freedom in prayer, accepts the Book of Common Prayer, as it was revised, proposed and recommended for use by the general convention of the Protestant Episcopal Church, A. D. 1785, reserving full liberty to alter, abridge, enlarge and amend the same, as may seem most conducive to the edification of the people, "provided that the substance of the faith be kept entire."

IV.

This Church condemns and rejects the following erroneous and strange doctrines as contrary to God's Word:

First, That the Church of Christ exists only in one order or form of ecclesiastical polity;

Second, That Christian ministers are "priests" in another sense than that in which all believers are "a royal priesthood;"

Third, That the Lord's Table is an altar on which the oblation of the Body and Blood of Christ is offered anew to the Father;

Fourth, That the Presence of Christ in the Lord's Supper is a presence in the elements of Bread and Wine;

Fifth, That Regeneration is inseparably connected with Baptism.

[Signed]
GEO. DAVID CUMMINS,
MARSHALL B. SMITH.
ALBERT CRANE,
GUSTAVUS A. SABINE,
CHARLES D. KELLOGG.

The Report of the Committee was then, on motion, unanimously adopted.

The PRESIDENT then rising, said: "By the unanimous votes of Ministers and Laymen present, I now declare that, on this second day of December, in the year of our Lord one thousand eight hundred and seventy-three, we have organized ourselves into a Church, to be known by the style and title of *The Reformed Episcopal Church,* conformable with the Declaration of Principles adopted this day, and with the Right Reverend George David Cummins, D.D., as our Presiding Bishop."

The Temporary President then retired, and the Bishop took the chair.

The BISHOP presiding then offered Prayer, after which he delivered an

ADDRESS ON THE PRAYER BOOK OF 1785.

From which we make the following extracts:

The Prayer Book of A. D. 1785, is the old path to which we return, and the basis upon which we take our stand at the beginning of our work. What is, then, the history of that book? and what are its claims to our regard? Let us answer these questions as briefly as possible.

In the month of September, 1783, the treaty of peace was signed at Paris, the consummation and reward of the seven long years of struggle and suffering of our Revolutionary Fathers to achieve their national independence. But even before this event, the Episcopal clergy, who had before the Revolution been known as Clergy of the Church of England, began to take measures looking to such an organization of their ecclesiastical system as was rendered necessary by the independence of the United States. The clergy of the State of Maryland seem to have been among the first move in this matter.

On the 13th day of August, 1783, a meeting or convention of the Episcopal clergy of the State of Maryland was held at Annapolis, moved thereto first, be it recorded, by a layman, William Paca, Governor of Maryland. That meeting or convention drew up a memorial or petition to the General Assembly of the State of Maryland, in which, as far as we are informed, occurs, for the first time in an official document, the title *The Protestant Episcopal Church.*

In May, 1784, the second step was taken towards the organization of the Protestant Episcopal Church in the United States. A few of the clergy of the States of New York, New Jersey and Pennsylvania, met at New Brunswick, N.

J., on the 13th and 14th of May, 1784, to confer together concerning the interests of the corporation for the support of widows and orphans of deceased clergymen. "Here," says Bishop White, "it was determined to procure a larger meeting on the 5th of the ensuing October, in the City of New York, not only for the purpose of reviving the said charitable institution, but to confer and agree on some general principles of an union of the Episcopal Church throughout the States."

On the 5th day of October, 1784, clergymen and laymen from eight States assembled in New York, and recommended "Seven principles of Ecclesiastical Union" as a basis for future organization. They also recommended that a convention, composed of clerical and lay deputies from the conventions of the different States, be convened in the City of Philadelphia, on the 27th of September, 1785.

On September 28th, the second day of the session, a committee was appointed to take the important work of revising the Prayer Book in hand, consisting of one clerical and one lay deputy from each State represented. The chairman of this committee of fourteen persons was the Rev. William Smith, D.D., of Maryland, formerly the Provost of the College and Academy of Philadelphia. It is believed that to him and to Bishop White we are chiefly indebted for the thorough revision accomplished in the Proposed Prayer Book set forth and recommended for use by that convention.

On the 5th day of October, 1785, the work of revision was finished, and the Liturgy ready for use; and on the same day the Convention passed the following resolution:

" WEDNESDAY EVENING, Oct. 5, 1785.

"*Ordered*, That the Rev. Dr. Smith be requested to prepare and preach a sermon suited to the solemn occasion of the present Convention, on Friday next; and that the Convention attend the same. and that *the services of the Church as proposed for future use, be then read for the first time.*"

The Liturgy, as thus revised, was read for the first time in public worship by the Rev. Wm. White, D. D.

The sermon preached on that occasion, by the Rev. Dr. Smith, I make the following extracts from:

This Prayer Book was printed first in Philadelphia in 1786, and reprinted in London in 1789, and the edition now before you is an exact reprint of the London edition of that year.

One other fact connected with the history of this remarkable book is to be recorded. The general convention of 1785 sent a petition to the Archbishops and Bishops of the Church of England, asking them to confer "the Episcopal character" on such presbyters as should be elected to that office by the several conventions of the States, and forwarded a copy of the proposed Prayer Book to them for their inspection. To this request the Archbishops and Bishops of the Church of England returned an answer encouraging the convention to hope for

CHICAGO

Young Men's Christian Association.

ORGANIZED, 1857.

JNO. V. FARWELL, *President.*   N. S. BOUTON, *Vice-President*
GEO. M. HIGH, *Secretary.*

FREE LIBRARY AND READING ROOMS,

No. 10 ARCADE COURT.

OPEN EVERY DAY FROM 8 A. M. TO 10 P. M.,

And a cordial invitation is extended to EVERYBODY to visit them.

OVER 100 PERIODICALS

Are on file, embracing many of the principal Secular, Religious
Literary, Pictorial, and Local Papers, and a large
selection of MAGAZINES.

FREE LIBRARY OF 2,700 VOLUMES!

Including works on Religion, Morality, Travel, History,
Biography, Science, Fiction, and Poetry.

MEETINGS AT THE ROOMS AS FOLLOWS:

Noonday Prayer Meeting,
Daily, at 12 M., for 45 minutes.

Young Men's Prayer Meeting,
Every Saturday Evening.

Conversational Bible Class,
Every Sunday, 9 A. M., for one hour.

Everybody's Sunday School,
Every Sunday, 3 P. M.

Gospel Meeting,
In Farwell Hall, every Sunday Eve'g.

Strangers' Meeting,
Every Monday Evening.

Young Men's Temperance Meeting,
Every Thursday Evening.

Lyceum,
Every Friday Evening.

Young men, especially strangers, are cordially invited to avail
themselves of these privileges. Free to all. The latch string is
always out. Come.

W. W. VANARSDALE, *Superintendent.*

success in their application, but objecting to some of the alterations in the proposed Prayer Book. The things objected to were only the rejection of the Nicene and Athanasian Creeds, and the clause, "He descended into hell," in the Apostles' Creed. No objection was offered to the other alterations. These exceptions taken by the English Bishops were received kindly, and at the meeting of the general convention in the next year, 1786, at Wilmington, Delaware, it was determined to restore the Nicene Creed and the omitted clause in the Apostles' Creed; but the proposition to restore the Athanasian Creed was almost unanimously rejected.

At the next triennial session of the general convention in 1789, most of the alterations in the proposed book failed to receive the sanction of that body, and the present Prayer Book of the Protestant Episcopal Church was adopted as it now stands, excepting the articles of religion, the ordinal, the office of institution, and the form of consecration of a church.

How different might have been the history and position to-day of that church, if the proposed Prayer Book had become the standard of its doctrine and worship! Still, the great fact remains that the proposed Prayer Book of 1785 bears with it the sanction, indorsement and recommendation, unanimous, as far as we know, of the wise, venerable and saintly men composing that convention. In returning to its use, we are only accepting their recommendation, and restoring "the old paths." What, then, are the chief points of difference between the two Prayer Books? They are substantially the following:

The words "Priest" and "Altar" are not to be found in the proposed book, and consequently, many now-called *priestly* acts are either omitted or devolved upon the officiating "minister;" thus, the present "Declaration of Absolution, or Remission of Sins, to be made by the Priest," etc., is simply "A declaration concerning the forgiveness of sins, to be made by the Minister," etc. So in the communion office, what is at present restricted to the Priest alone, as placing upon the table "so much bread and wine as he shall think sufficient," etc., is made the duty of " the minister."

The difference in the baptismal services is very marked. In that for children the words in the address of the Minister, " Seeing now, dearly beloved brethren, that this child is regenerate, and grafted into the body of Christ's Church," are not found in the proposed book ; and the collect, which reads, " We give, thee hearty thanks, most merciful Father, that it hath pleased thee *to regenerate this infant with thy Holy Spirit*, to receive him for thy own child by adoption," etc., is in the proposed book, without the words in italics. In the address to the sponsors, instead of, "Wherefore, * * * this infant, must also faithfully, for his part, promise by you that are his sureties (until he comes of age to take it upon himself), that he will renounce the devil and all his works, and constantly believe God's holy word, and obediently keep His commandments." The proposed book reads thus: " Wherefore, * * * you must also faithfully,

HOUSES

AT

NORTH EVANSTON!

TO RENT AND FOR SALE

CHEAP

AND ON

Easy Terms.

Will build to suit Customers and give long time on payments.

GROVE LOTS

25x150 Feet,

FOR

$150

ON

MONTHLY PAYMENTS.

JOHN CULVER,

Southwest Corner Clark and Washington Sts.

for your part, promise and answer to the following questions (which take the place of those now in the service), viz.:

Minister.—"Dost thou believe all the articles of the Christian faith as contained in the Apostles' Creed, and wilt thou endeavor to have this child instructed accordingly?"

Answer.—"I do believe them, and by God's help will endeavor so to do."

A corresponding modification of the questions is found in the order for adult baptism. Of course, this peculiar phraseology of the services involved corresponding changes in the Catechism, the Catechism answering the question, as to whom he received his name—"I received it in baptism when I *became a member of the Christian Church,*" instead of "a member of Christ, a child of God, and an inheritor of the kingdom of heaven." As to what was promised for him in baptism, he is to say: "That I should be instructed in all the articles of the Christian faith as contained in the Apostles' Creed, and brought up," etc. In answer to the subsequent question, "Why, then, are infants baptized," etc., he is to say, "Because their sureties promise to instruct them."

The Confirmation Service was modified so as to make the inquiries addressed to the candidates correspond with these alterations; and the first prayer, in the same office, was changed to exclude from it an endorsement of the doctrine of invariable regeneration in baptism.

The Nicene Creed has not been retained; and the clause, "He descended into hell," is omitted from the Apostles' Creed, which, as is said in a note in the preface of the book, Bishop Burnet, Bishop Pearson, and other writers inform us, is found in no creed, nor mentioned by any writer, until about the beginning of the fifth century.

These are the chief alterations made in the Prayer Book by the Convention of 1785, as far as they affect doctrine; but other and less important improvements and additions were made. The repetition of the Gloria Patri, at the end of every psalm, being classed among "the unnecessary repetitions of the same prayers or subject matter, is not allowed. Some changes were made in the chants and anthems, omitting the *Benedicite*, and retaining the chants entitled the *Magnificat* and *Nunc Dimittis* in the Evening Prayer, as in the English Prayer Book. A Special Service is introduced for the 4th of July, and the whole Liturgy is imbued with a spirit of fervent patriotism that distinguished the men of that memorable period of our history.

Is the Prayer Book of 1785, then, perfect? free form objection? By no means. Nothing human is free from imperfection. But this we claim, that since the beginning of the Reformation of the sixteenth century, no prayer book has ever yet been set forth so unexceptionable and so near conformity to Holy Scripture. We accept it as a precious boon left to us from our fathers, older than the Constitution of the United States, and dating back to the very infancy of our existence as a nation. But we reserve to ourselves full liberty to amend, alter

SIMEON W. KING,

ATTORNEY AT LAW, NOTARY PUBLIC,

U. S. COURT COMMISSIONER,

For Northern District of Illinois.

COMMISSIONER OF DEEDS

For ALL the STATES and TERRITORIES, to wit.:

Alabama,	Idaho,	Maine,	Pennsylvania.
Alaska,	Illinois,	Minnesota,	Rhode Island,
Arizona,	Indiana,	Montana,	South Carolina.
Arkansas,	Iowa,	New York,	Tennessee,
California,	Kansas,	New Jersey,	Texas,
Colorado,	Kentucky,	New Hampshire,	Utah,
Connecticut,	Louisiana,	North Carolina,	Vermont,
Dakota,	Massachusetts,	Nebraska,	Virginia,
Delaware,	Maryland,	New Mexico,	West Virginia,
Dist. Columbia,	Michigan,	Nevada,	Wisconsin,
Florida,	Mississippi,	Ohio,	Washington,
Georgia,	Missouri,	Oregon,	Wyoming.

Commissioner for the U. S. Court of Claims and Passport Officer.

Deeds, &c., drawn according to the law where recorded or used, and properly acknowledged. Depositions and Affidavits taken for use in any State, Federal, Territorial, Canadian or European Court. Passports obtained, Marine Protests Entered, **Insurance Statements Sworn and Certified to.** Notes protested. Accounts and Past Due Claims prepared for collection and verified. *Proofs in Bankrupt proceedings drawn, proven up, and certified, same as before a Register in Bankruptcy.*

Office, Methodist Church Block,

⌐ROOM 3,⌐

Cor. Clark & Washington Streets,   CHICAGO.

U. S. COMMISSIONER'S COURT held by Mr. King at his office. Jurisdiction in all matter pertaining to violation of Revenue Laws or any Crime committed against the Government.

Mr. King is the ONLY *Commissioner of Deeds* in Chicago (if not in the United States) who has *a separate Official Seal of Office for each State and Territory,* AS REQUIRED BY LAW. Legal Business of every description promptly attended to.

enlarge or abridge this book, as the Lord may guide us by His Holy Spirit. Nor do we purpose to make this Liturgy so imperative or obligatory on the con-sciences of men that it is always and only to be used, or that freedom in prayer is to be denied and repressed. We thankfully accept this book from our fa-thers. We will alter, amend, abridge or enlarge it only with great caution and discretion, and asking the guidance of the blessed Spirit.

This, then, is our attitude towards our brethren of the Protestant Episcopal Church. We are not schismatics (no man can be a schismatic who does not deny the faith); we are restorers of the old; repairers of the breaches; reform-ers. And, as in Israel of old, when the tribes of Reuben and of Gad and the half tribe of Manasseh, returning to their inheritance on the eastern side of Jordan, in the fullness of their gratitude, had built there an altar, "a great altar to see to;" and when the other tribes of Israel, moved with great indignation, "gathered themselves at Shiloh to go up to war against them." "the children of Reuben and the children of Gad, and the half tribe of Manasseh, answered and said unto the heads of the thousands of Israel: The Lord God of gods—the Lord God of gods—he knoweth, and Israel he shall know, if it be in *rebellion* or transgression against the Lord, save us not this day—that we have built us an altar to turn from following the Lord; but that it may be a witness between us and you, and our generations after us, that we might do the service of the Lord before him, with our burnt-offerings, and with our sacrifices, and with our peace-offerings ; that your children may not say to our children, in time to come: Ye have no part in the Lord—wherefore, said we, that it shall be, when they should so say to us or to our generations in time to come, that we may say again, Behold the pattern of the altar of the Lord, which our fathers made, not for burnt-offerings, nor for sacrifices; but it is a witness between us and you ;—and the thing pleased the children of Israel; and the children of Israel blessed God and did not intend to go up against them in battle, to destroy the land wherein the children of Reuben and Gad dwelt;"—so declare we now to our brethren, who with great indignation have lifted up their voices against us; and to those who raise the hand of human might to overwhelm us: the Lord God of gods, and the Lord Jesus Christ—the "Head over all things to His Church"—He know-eth, and all His people shall know, that not in rebellion or in transgression against the Lord have we done this thing, but that it may be a witness between us and you, and our generations after us, "that your children may not say to our children in time to come, Ye have no part in the Lord. The Lord our God judge between us and you."

Towards all other Christian people, of like precious faith, our attitude is that only of love, of sympathy, and of earnest desire to co-operate with them in the extension of the kingdom of the Redeemer—both theirs and ours. We re-gard our movement only as a step towards the closer union of all Evangelical Christendom. For this we shall labor and pray. We gladly acknowledge the

FROM SWORN RETURNS.

Sewing Machine Sales of 1874,

COMPARISON WITH SALES OF 1873.

	1874.	1873.
The Singer Manufacturing Co., sold	241,679	232,444
Wheeler & Wilson Manf'g Co., sold	92,827	119,190
Howe Machine Co., estimated	35,000	No returns
Domestic Sewing Machine Co., sold	22,700	40,114
Weed Sewing Machine Co., sold	20,495	21,769
Grover & Baker Sewing Machine Co., sold	20,000	36,179
Remington Empire Sewing Machine Co., sold.	17,608	9,183
Wilson Sewing Machine Co., sold	17,525	21,247
Gold Medal Sewing Machine Co., sold	15,214	16,431
Wilcox & Gibbs Sewing Machine Co., sold	13,710	15,881
American B. H. Co., sold	13,529	14,182
Victor Sewing Machine Co., sold	6,292	7,446
Florence Sewing Machine Co., sold	5,517	8,960
Secor Sewing Machine Co., sold	4,541	4,430
.Etna, J. E. Braunsdorf & Co., sold	1,866	3,081
Bartram & Fanton, sold	250	1,000
McKay Sewing Machine Association, sold	128	....
Keystone Sewing Machine Co., sold	37	217

Facts beyond Controversy.   Comment unnecessary.

THE SINGER MANF'G CO.,

Western Office.   111 State Street, Chicago.

validity of the ministerial orders of our brethren whom God has sent into His vineyard, and whose labors He has accepted and blessed. We shall invite all ministers of Evangelical Churches to occupy our pulpits, and to take part in our services. And we shall rejoice to meet them and their flocks as often as may be expedient around the Lord's Table, and acknowledge that "we, being many, are one Body in Christ, and members of one another."

ELECTION OF BISHOP CHENEY.

On the 2d day of December, 1873, the Rev. Charles Edward Cheney, D.D., was elected Missionary Bishop of the Church and was consecrated as such Bishop in Christ Church, Chicago, Dec. 11, by Bishop Cummins.

The second General Council of the Church was held in the City of New York, beginning Wednesday, May 13, 1874, at 10½ A. M.

Bishop George David Cummins, D. D., was elected Presiding Bishop, and Herbert B. Turner as Secretary.

The third General Council was held in Christ Church, in the City of Chicago, commencing Wednesday, May 12, and ending Tuesday, May 18, 1875.

Bishop Cummins was elected Presiding Bishop, and Herbert B. Turner, Secretary.

Rev. Dr. Thompson, the delegate appointed by the General Synod of the Reformed Church in America to bear the Christian salutations of that body to the General Council, delivered an eloquent and interesting address before the Council on Friday morning. May 14.

Articles of federative union of the Free Church of England with the Reformed Episcopal Church were presented as having been ratified by the Free Church of England. Seven missionary jurisdictions were created by the Council, viz., the Missionary jurisdictions of St. John, of Ottawa, of the Pacific, of the East, the Central Missionary jurisdiction, the Missionary jurisdiction of the South, and of the West and Northwest. The Rev. Edward Cridge, B.A. Oxon, of Victoria, British Columbia. the Rev. Jas. A. Latane, of Virginia, and the Rev. Wm. R. Nicholson. D.D., of Philadelphia, were elected Missionary Bishops on Monday, May 17th.

The Articles of Religion were adopted at this Council on the 15th of May.

SYNODICAL COUNCIL.

On the 28th of September the first Synodical Council of the Church was held at St. Paul's Church, Chicago. Delegates were present from Christ Church, St. Paul's Church, Church of the Good Shepherd, Emmanuel Church, North Side, Immanuel Church, South Side, Chicago; Christ Church, Peoria, and the Reformed Episcopal Church at Chillicothe.

The delegates from St. Paul were, A. M. Wright, J. W. Bennett. F. A. Bryau. O. B. Sansum, L. J, Colburn, E. P. Brooks, Prof. M. L. Rogers.

The first Synodical Council of the Reformed Episcopal Church was held at St. Paul's Church, Tuesday, September 28, 1875.

THE

Good Samaritan

SOCIETY, OF CHICAGO,

Was Organized to give to Girls and Women who are without employment, home, or friends, a helping hand, sympathy and Counsel.

THE INDUSTRIAL HOME,

74 Grant Place, near Lincoln Park,

Was opened September 5th, 1874, for tho purpose of furnishing the unemployed workingmen of the city with a temporary home and industrial training. Board is also furnished to the empolyed, at a nominal price, the price in all cases to be determined by the means of the applicant. Instruction is given in the Musical Department, and sewing is done in the Sewing Department at reduced rates. In the Laundry, plain family washing and ironing is done for 75 cents per dozen. Orders should be addressed, and applications for admission to the Home should be made to the Office of the Society.

Room 14, 171 & 173 E. Randolph St.

All persons interested in the progress of the work are invited to visit the Home and down-town Office of the Association. Regular meetings for the transaction of business and admission of members will be held the first Thursday of each month. Strangers always welcome.

Mrs. ANNIE E. WALBERT, Pre's.

Mrs. T. J. BLUTHARDT, *Vice-Presidents.*
Mrs. HERMAN RASTER,

M rs E. W. SPALDING, *Treasurer.*   **Mrs. E. C. BAKER,** *Secretary.*

A. M. Wright, Esq., was chosen temporary President, and W. A. Beasly, Esq., of Peoria, temporary Secretary. The Synod was termed the Synod of Chicago. L. P. Morehouse was elected permanent Secretary, F. J. Birnay was elected Treasurer, Bishop Cheney, D. D., was elected Synodical Bishop, which position was accepted.

STANDING COMMITTEE.—The Rev. Samuel Fallows, D. D., the Rev. J. D. Wilson, the Rev. Wm. H. Cooper, D. D., A. M. Wright, Esq., Alexander Tyng, Esq. and R. Cole, Esq., were elected the Standing Committee by the Synod.

DELEGATES.—The following persons were elected delegates to the synodical council from St. Paul's Church: A. M. Wright, delegate at large, Col. J. W. Bennett, P. R. Westfall, F. A. Bryan, L. J. Colburn, W. M. Lewis, O. B. Sansum. W. G. Thompson and E. P. Brooks.

ALTERNATES.—John Gilman, Prof. M. L. Rogers, E. W. Westfall, John Fairbanks, G. W. Rainey.

Bishop Chas. Edward Cheney, D. D., was elected Synodical Bishop.

The Council adjourned to meet on the first Tuesday in April, 1876, at 10 a. m., in St. Paul's Church, Chicago.

The Reformed Episcopal Church now numbers about 60 ministers and churches and 10,000 communicants. Its growth has been remarkable considering the short period since its organization.

THE APPEAL

is the name of the newspaper published monthly in the interests of the Reformed Episcopal Church, and was issued January 1, 1876. The following names compose its editorial staff:

SAMUEL FALLOWS, D.D., Editor-in-Chief. Associate Editors: Bishop George David Cummins, D. D., Bishop Charles Edward Cheney, D. D., Rev. Marshall B. Smith, Passaic, N. J., Rev. W. H. Cooper, D. D., Chicago, Rev W. M. Postlethwaite, Baltimore, Md., Rev. H. M. Collisson, Ottawa, Ont., Rev. Joseph D. Wilson, Peoria, Ill.

Edward P. Brooks & Co. are the publishers. 76 Monroe st.

The paper has received the highest recommendations from the press, and has been warmly received by the whole church. It is receiving constantly large lists of subscribers. The subscription price is only $1.00 per year.

THE "UNIVERSITY OF THE WEST"

is the name of the first University of the Reformed Episcopal Church, which is soon to be established at or near Chicago.

The following extract from the Chicago *Tribune* will give an idea of the plan of the University:

In regard to the proposed University of the West for the Reformed Episcopal Church, the following information has been obtained by a *Tribune* reporter: The Board of Trustees has at present under consideration a number of suggestions and ideas, and are receiving bids from suburban towns which want

MOVEMENT CURE,
For the Treatment of Chronic Diseases.
IS LOCATED AT
105 & 107 STATE STREET,
(Southeast Cor. State and Washington).

The Modern developments of the Movement Cure supplement the ordinary manipulations and processes by the *unique* and *ingenious* application of **MECHANICAL APPARATUS**, in great variety of form (propelled by steam power), capable of supplying Rubbings, Frictions, Kneadings, Oscillations, etc., in the most agreeable and effective manner.

It is a remedial method, for which there is no adequate substitute; affording new hope to the invalid, being alike suited to his understanding and to his disease. This system of treatment is eminently medical, and commands the respect of medical men and the patronage of the most intelligent and influential people of this City.

We have seventeen years' experience in this special field of practice (the past nine years in this city), and have the most spacious, best fitted, and most successful Movement Cure in the United States. Send for Circular.   J. G. TRINE, M. D.

Campbell,
146 State St.,
Importer and Manufacturer
of all kinds of
HAIR GOODS.

HAIR JEWELRY made to ORDER
Tools, Materials, Molds and Gold Mountings
Constantly on hand for the trade.

WIGS, TOUPEES, FRONTS, ETC.,
And every article belonging to the Wig Trade at Wholesale.
Campbell's Japanese Hair Dye,
The only Brown Dye in the World. Try it and you will never do without it.

to have the buildings located in their midst. Among these are Washington Heights, Morgan Park, Hinsdale, South Englewood, Hawthorn, Glencoe, and Thornton. These all make liberal propositions, and the Trustees are considering them, but it is not yet known where the University will be located.

The scope of the University will naturally be vast, as there will be but one for the entire denomination in the West; all other institutions of learning will be colleges or seminaries, wherever they may be located. The faculties of these several colleges will be a portion of the faculty of the University.

Another feature will be that, under this regulation, the University alone can confer degrees. The courses of study and examination, in all like grades of this institution, or its colleges, will also be alike, and thus give the best features of Oxford and Cambridge Universities.

It is well known that every denomination has organized a number of colleges under different charters, which has, in many instances, proven a grave mistake and led to financial failures. Nearly every denomination has seen the mistake of multiplying colleges with separate charters and full academic powers, and has realized the great necessity of having a grand central university, organically related to the several colleges.

The Reformed Episcopal University of the West proposes to profit by the mistakes of other denominations, and is the first to put into realization in this country the full meaning of the true University idea. Another feature will be the conferring of the higher degrees upon examination alone—such as Doctor of Philosophy, Doctor of Divinity, Doctor of Laws, etc., following the plan of the London and better German Universities. This plan was first inaugurated by Dr. Fallows, in the Illinois Wesleyan University at Bloomington, and worked admirably and with marked success. Several gentlemen have passed brilliant examinations for the several degrees, as ministers, and clergymen, and professors in colleges. This feature makes the conferring of degrees one of absolute merit, and not of favor, as has been the case, as is well known, in many instances. The examinations of the University will be conducted by gentlemen eminent for their scholarship, who, in conjunction with the faculty, will constitute the Board of Examiners.

Examinations will be in writing. This plan, also, has met with marked favor from the leading educators of the country, as an entirely new feature in American collegiate history. Wherever the University may be located, there will be grouped around it colleges of theology, law, medicine, music, technology, the sciences and the arts. This will be one of its crowning features, and will be carried on in a manner heretofore almost unknown in this country. A complete education in the fine arts may be secured here from competent professors. The musical academy will also be placed on a model basis, and the curriculum will include everything from the teaching of mere piano playing to the full and highest culture of the voice.

The financial basis has been provided for by the University. The point at which it is located, of course, will give a handsome donation in lands and money. Lands will also be purchased by the University corporation as required, and it is expected that liberal donations will be made for the endowment of chairs in individual colleges. A great many friends of the University stand ready to give land, which will, undoubtedly, prove of great value in years to come.

There is one thing that should be especially noted. The University is going to avoid the terrible rock upon which so many institutions of learning have split—the great rock of debt. The Trustees propose first to endow living men, and not a dead pile of brick stone and mortar. They intend to first put up a wing of a very handsome and commodious building, and put up the main structure

so soon as practicable. All the necessary funds to carry on the enterprise will be forthcoming when it is decided where the University shall be located.

The following persons have been appointed Trustees:

Bishop Charles E. Cheney, D D.,   Rev. Samuel Fallows, D. D.,
Rev. Joseph D. Wilson.   Rev. Malcolm McCormick,
Rev. J. P. Davis,   Rev. Willis H. Cooper, D. D.,
Rev. Ernst Guntrum.   Rev. Albert Walkley,
F. A. Bryan,   William Aldrich.
A. M. Wright,   Samuel Beers,
E. St. John.   Elbridge G. Keith.
James Whyte,   Wm. E. Wheeler,
Alexander G. Tyng,   James N. Hyde, M. D.
L. J. Colburn,   Gurdon S. Hubbard,
E. B. Phillipps.   J. W. Bennett.

Ex-Officio Members.

The Governor of the State of Illinois,
The Supt. of Public Instruction of Illinois,
Supt. of Public Instruction of Chicago,
The Presiding Bishop of Ref. E. Church, and
The Chancellor of the University.

THE

Hershey School

OF

MUSICAL ART,

42 S. Ann Street, Chicago,

Opposite First Congregational Church.

A new institution established for the study of *Instrumental and Vocal* music from the beginning to the *most advanced* stages of progress; but more especially to afford young ladies who have finished their ordinary school routine an opportunity of pursuing the higher branches of Musical Art as well as the Modern Languages and Elocution.

None but the best teachers employed.

Pupils can enter at any time.

Send for Circular.

DIRECTORS:

W. S. B. MATHEWS, Instrumental.

MRS. SARA B. HERSHEY, Vocal.

By permission refer to Samuel Fallows, D. D.

BRIEF SKETCH

OF

ST. PAUL'S CHURCH HISTORY.

The Rt. Rev. Charles Edward Cheney, Missionary of the West and Northwest, true to that indefatigable zeal and unfaltering energy that has so conspicuously marked his career, commenced early in January, 1875, holding one service each Sunday in the West Division of our city. This movement was begun with the view of eventually establishing an organization under the auspices of the Reformed Episcopal Church of which he was the acknowledged founder and recognized ecclesiastical leader in the West. These efforts of the Bishop, begun under circumstances that would beget discouragement in one imbued with a lesser degree of fortitude, were fraught with results surpassing the predictions of the most sanguine disciples and proselytes to the new organization. The associate rector, the Rev. Wm. M. Postlethwaite, ably assisted Bishop Cheney in these ministrations until the 14th of February following, when the congregation resolved to effect a permanent organization. In compliance with this unanimous resolve the Bishop appointed the following named gentlemen: John Walker, John W. Bennett, H. P. Merrill, E. St. John, and George W. Rainey, a committee empowered to effect arrangements sufficient unto the requirements of the newly formed congregation.

The first duty devolving upon the committee was to select quarters other than those then occupied, for the old St. John's Church on

Lake Street, opposite Union Park, was by far too small and inconveniently located to accommodate the rapidly increasing congregation. This unpretending edifice, hallowed by the labors of one so eminent in ability, so devotedly earnest and untiring in the Master's Work as was the late Rev. H. N. Powers, D. D., was relinquished for the building now occupied on Washington street, near the corner of Ann.

In the meantime a call had been extended to the Rev. Samuel Fallows, D. D., President of the Wesleyan University of Bloomington, Illinois, who had, years before, mapped out as the true church of the future what he then saw suddenly and unexpectedly springing into a healthy existence under the name of the Reformed Episcopal Church. After the most prayerful consideration the Doctor accepted the call, and in the month of June last formally entered upon his duties as pastor of this infant church.

The Sunday-school was organized in April last, with about twenty scholars, with neither books, papers, nor class-cards,—in a word, with nothing but loving hearts and willing hands, ready to work for the advancement of the youthful members of the church. Verily, much good often results from small beginnings, for our Sunday-school has increased with a rapidity exceeding the expectations of the most sanguine. No sudden transitory increase consequent upon a temporary excitement, but a strong, earnest and enduring interest, has resulted in securing 260 scholars and a well-selected library of some 300 volumes, and all the appurtenances necessary and convenient.

Thus it will be seen that St. Paul's Church is firmly established upon a basis that promises much for the future. This compendium would be imperfect were it not to state that much of the success of St. Paul's Church depends upon her faithful, enthusiastic pastor, who is not only greatly esteemed by those who find enjoyment and profit under his loving and intelligent ministrations, but by every member of the community who is acquainted with him. Moreover, it should ever be remembered that in resigning the presidency of

the University at Bloomington, Dr. Fallows threw up a lucrative position, one with less labor and greater remuneration, in order to carry out the fond work of his choice.

ST. PAUL'S R. E. CHURCH.

HOURS OF SERVICE.

Sundays...10:30 a. m.
From Easter to October 1st,........................ 7:45 p. m
From October 1st to Easter,.........................7:30 p. m.

WEDNESDAYS.

Prayer Meeting and Bible Class.
From October 1st till Easter.......................7:30 p. m.
" Easter to October 1st..........................7:45 p. m.

Communion on the first Sunday of every month at the morning service.

Baptism can be had on any Sunday, either at church service or Sunday-school, by giving previous notice.

SUNDAY SCHOOL

Is held in the church parlors at 3 o clock p. m.

The rector, the Rev. Samuel Fallows, D.D., resides at No. 530 Fulton St. and will gladly visit, by appointment or otherwise, any persons wishing to see him about religious matters.

Pews can be rented from Mr. A. M. Wright, Mr. J. W. Bennett, or the Treasurer, Mr. F. A. Bryan, after any service.

The sexton, Mr. Putman, resides at 268 W. Harrison.

THE CHOIR

of St. Paul's Church has ever been an attractive and notable feature, and those who are fond of good music could not help being pleased in this particular. The pastor tries in every way to encourage congregational singing, believing that praise is as essential as prayer and should be participated in by all.

Organist—Mr. C. C. Coffin.

Manager—Mr. C. C. Lefler; and Mrs. M. M. Dutton, Miss Jessie Hardy and Mr. C. F. Claxton, compose the balance of the choir.

Of the individual merits of each of the above members it is quite unnecessary to comment.

CHURCH OFFICERS.

Elected April 5, 1875; term of service, one year.

A. M. Wright—Senior Warden.

J. W. Bennett—Junior Warden.

E. St. John—Secretary.

VESTRYMEN.

ELECTED APRIL 5th, 1875.

John Walker,
R. S. Whitcomb, } For three years.
F. A. Bryan.

H. Eddy,
E. St. John, } For two years.
H. P. Merrill.

G. W. Raney,
C. W. Castle, } For one year.
L. J. Colburn.

G. T. CARPENTER,

DOCTOR OF

Dental Surgery,

GRADUATE OF

The Pennsylvania College of Dental Surgery, Philadelphia.

OFFICE AND RESIDENCE :

NO. 444 WEST LAKE STREET,

CORNER OF ADA.

Dentistry in all its Branches,

Special attention given to the

TREATMENT OF DISEASE AND SURGERY OF THE MOUTH

AND ASSOCIATE PARTS.

Also, the Care and Corrections of Irregularity of Children's Teeth.

Dr. Carpenter's

TOOTH POWDER AND MOUTH WASHES

FOR SALE AT HIS OFFICE,

No. 444 WEST LAKE STREET,

Corner of Ada,   CHICAGO.

Church Congregation—Residences.

A.

Adams, W. C.,	Tremont House.
Adams, Sarah A.,	9 S. Peoria st.
Allen, John,	245 Walnut st.
Allen, Mrs. John,	245 Walnut st.
Allen, John, Jr.,	245 Walnut st.
Allen, Joseph,	245 Walnut st.
Alexander, Hm., Jr.,	1018 Wilcox ave.
Armstrong, A.,	116 W. Washington st.
Armstrong, Mrs. J.,	401 W. Jackson st.
Armstrong, Miss K.,	401 W. Jackson st.
Arnold, Mrs. C. M.,	259 W. 13th st.
Ackley, F. D.,	19 N. Carpenter st.
Ackley, Mrs. F. D.,	19 N. Carpenter st.
Ackley, Miss Ina L.	19 N. Carpenter st.
Atkinson, J. C.,	51 Ashland ave.

B.

Ball, George,	Clifton House.
Ball, John,	Clifton House.
Bankson, M., Mrs.	733 W. Lake st.
Bash, F. S.,	70 S. Morgan st.
Baxter, Mrs.,	638 Warren ave.
Beach, Miss H. W.,	457 W. Jackson st.
Bears, M.,	418 W. Jackson st.
Bears, Mrs. C. J.,	418 W. Jackson st.
Bears, Chas. G.,	46 St. John's Place.
Bellamy, Mrs. Sarah J.,	567 Fulton st.
Bennett, Col. J. W.,	45 S. Ashland ave.
Bennett, Mrs. Col. J. W.,	45 S. Ashland ave.

I. A. FREEMAN, Dentist, 468 Randolph St., Cor. Sheldon St.

Bennett, Miss M. A., ... 45 S. Ashland ave.
Benson, Dr. J. W., . . . 631 York st.
Benson, Miss Cora, ... 631 York st.
Benson, Miss Bertha, . . . 631 York st.
Benson, Miss Ada, ... 631 York st.
Benson, Miss Nellie, . . . 631 York st.
Benson, Master Chas., . . . 631 York st.
Benson, Master R. Lee, . . . 631 York st.
Bishop, Frank, ... 106 Dearborn st.
Bishop, Fred. A. . . . 378 W. Madison st.
Bird, J. A. F., ... 23 Irving Place.
Bird, Mrs. J. A. F., . . . 23 Irving Place.
Bouton, Miss E. S., . . . 296 W. Monroe st.
Boyle, Miss, ... 56 Ann st.
Boynton, Mrs., ...
Bradshaw, J. H., ... 89 Warren ave.
Bradshaw, Mrs. J. H., . . . 89 Warren ave.
Brannan, Miss Bessie M., . . . 42 S. Ann st.
Brooks, Edward P., ... Hyde Park.
Brooks, Mrs. Helen M., . . . Hyde Park.
Brown, Jno., ...
Brown, J. B., . . . 136 W. Jackson st.
Brown, Ira, . . . 393 W. Randolph st.
Brown, Mrs. Ira, . . . 393 W. Randolph st.
Bryan, F. A., ... 1 Bryan Place.
Bryan, Miss Grace M., . . . 1 Bryan Place.
Bryan, A. C., ... 1 Bryan Place.
Bryan, H. A., . . . 1 Bryan Place.
Bryan, F. W., ... 681 Warren ave.
Bryan, Mrs. F. W., . . . 681 Warren ave.

C.

Campbell, Mrs., - - - - Cor. Lake and Paulina.
Campbell, F., - - - - 92 S. Ashland ave.
Campbell, Mrs. F., - - - - 92 S. Ashland ave.

JAMES W. MILL,

PHARMACEUTICAL CHEMIST,

DEALER IN

Pure Medicines, Toilet Goods, Swedish Leeches,
Pure Liquors (for Medicinal use), Trusses,
Mineral Waters, Etc.,

572 WEST MADISON STREET, COR. OGDEN AVENUE.

BRANCH STORE.   ESTABLISHED 1860.   MILL & GOODMAN.
654 W. Van Buren.   133 S. Halsted.

J. ROGERSON,

UNDERTAKER,

487 WEST MADISON & 113 WEST RANDOLPH STS.,

CHICAGO.

Funerals furnished in every style.

ESTABLISHED 1859.

Wm. L. Harcourt,

Prescription Druggist,

No. 366 W. MADISON STREET.

(NEAR ANN ST.).

CHICAGO.

Carlton, K.,   -   -   -   -   - 438 Hubbard st.
Carpenter, Mrs. J.,   -   -   -   -   - 56 Walnut st.
Carpenter, Miss E. M., -   -   -   - 21 St. John's Place.
Carpenter, Eli,   -   -   -   - 21 St. John's Place.
Carpenter, F. W. -   -   -   -   11 N. Sangamon st.
Carpenter, Mrs. F. W., -   -   -   11 N. Sangamon st.
Carpenter, G. T., Dentist, -   -   - 444 W. Lake st.
Carpenter, Mrs. G. T., -   -   -   444 W. Lake st.
Carpenter, Ira,   -   -   -   - 627 W. Lake st.
Carpenter, Miss Emma,   -   -   -   627 W. Lake st.
Carr, Dr., W.   -   -   -   -   -   46 S. May st.
Carr, Mrs. Dr., -   -   -   -   -   - 46 S. May st.
Costello, Mrs.,   -   -   -   -   - 409 Kinzie st.
Castle, C. W.,   -   -   -   -   - 403 S. Leavitt st.
Castle, Mrs. C. W.,   -   -   -   - 403 S. Leavitt st.
Castle, Chas. H., -   -   -   -   403 S. Leavitt st.
Chisholm, E. A,   -   -   -   -   - 9 Irving Place.
Chisholm, Mrs. E. A.,   -   -   -   - 9 Irving Place.
Chisholm, Mrs. H., -   -   -   -
Chase, Herbert,   -   -   -   -   - 21 Centre st.
Chase, Mrs. Herbert, -   -   -   -   21 Centre st.
Church, M. D., -   -   -   -   - St. Caroline Court.
Clark, Miss Mary, -   -   -   -   - 71 Park ave.
Clark, Miss Belle, -   -   -   -   - 71 Park ave.
Clow, Miss E.,   -   -   -   -   - 607 Fulton st.
Colburn, Levi J., -   -   .   .   - 71 Park ave.
Colburn, Mrs. Levi J., -   -   -   - 71 Park ave.
Coles, Miss Jennie, -   -   -   -   71 Park ave.
Coffin, C. C.,   -   -   -   -   - 297 Walnut st.
Colburn, Mrs.,   -   -   -   -   - 297 Walnut st.
Cox, Wm. G.,   -   -   -   -   - 352 Ohio st.
Cox, Mrs. Wm. G., -   -   -   -   - 352 Ohio st.
Cox, Fred., -   -   -   -   -   - 352 Ohio st.
Cox, W. G. Jr.,   -   -   -   -   225 Ohio st.
Cox, Miss Louise A.,   -   -   -   - 352 Ohio st.

THIRTY-SECOND

SEMI-ANNUAL STATEMENT

OF THE

HOME

LIFE INSURANCE COMPANY,

254 BROADWAY, NEW YORK.

JANUARY 1st, 1876.

Assets January 1st, 1875	$4,113,139 23
Premiums received in 1875....................	741,665 88
Interest	278,241 06
	$5,133,046 17
Ratio of Commission paid to Premiums received in 1875.......................................	8 06
Total amount of losses paid since organization.....	$2,080,394 00
Total amount of Interest received.................	1,925,491 00
Ratio of total Interest received to total losses paid..	92 57
Total amount of Dividends paid to Policy-holders..	1,738,637 00
Ratio of Interest received to losses paid in 1875....	1 21

Agents can obtain a very liberal contract with the Home by applying to

E. H. KELLOGG, Superintendent of Agencies,

METHODIST CHURCH BLOCK,

Chicago, Ill.

I take pleasure in referring to REV. SAMUEL FALLOWS, D. D., who has been insured in the Home since the first year of its organization.

E. H. KELLOGG.

Cox, Miss Augusta,   -   -   -   -   352 Ohio st.
Coyne, James H.,   -   -   -   -   - 216 Ogden ave.
Coyne, Mrs. James H., -   -   -   -   -   216 Ogden ave.
Coyne, Miss M. E.,   -   -   -   -   - 216 Ogden ave.
Crane, Mrs.,   -   -   -   -   -   18 Throop st.
Crane, E.,   -   -   -   -   307 W. Washington st.
Crane, C. R.,   -   -   -   - 369 W. Washington st.
Cummings, Miss L.,   -   -   -   373 W. Monroe st.
Cummings, Miss Lizzie,   -   -   -   - 373 W. Monroe st.

D.

Dart, Wm.,   -   -   -   -   318 W. Madison st.
Dart, Mrs. Elizabeth   -   -   -   318 W. Madison st.
Davison, Mrs. B. F.,   -   -   -   192 N. Carpenter st.
Davy, Miss Louisa,   -   -   -   -   781 Ada st.
Dorenberg, Miss M.,   -   -   -   42 Union Park Place.
Deering, Dr., -   -   -   -   -   - 427 Carroll ave.
Deering, Mrs. Dr.,   -   .   -   -   427 Carroll ave.
Dryer, Mrs.,   -   -   -   -   343 W. Washington st.
Dutton, Mrs. M. M.,   -   -   -   354 Van Buren st.
Duncan, Mrs. A.,   -   -   -   172 W. Washington st.

E.

Earll, D. S.,   -   -   -   383 W. Madison, cor. Green.
Earll, Mrs. D. S., -   -   383 W. Madison, cor. Green.
Eckhart, B. A.,   -   -   -   -   - 9 Bryan Place.
Eckhart, Mrs. B. A.,   -   -   -   -   9 Bryan Place.
Eddy, D. C.,   -   -   -   -   -   711 Fulton st.
Eddy, Mrs. D. C.,   -   -   -   -   - 711 Fulton st.
Emmons, Miss Kate, -   -   -   -   189 Madison st.

F.

Farovid, J. A.,   -   -   -   -   -   - 51 Curtis st.
Farovid, Mrs. J. A.,   -   -   -   -   -   - 51 Curtis st.
Fairbanks, Jno.,   -   -   -   -   710 W. Monroe st.
Fairbanks, Mrs. J.,   -   -   -   - 710 W. Monroe st.

CHICAGO

Musical College,

F. ZIEGFELD,   LOUIS FALK,
PRESIDENT.   *DIRECTOR.*

COLLEGE BUILDING,

295 & 297 W. Madison Street.

BRANCHES OF INSTRUCTION.
Piano, Singing, Organ, Harmony and Composition,
Instrumentation, Violin, Violencello, Flute,
Guitar, Etc.

MODERN LANGUAGES.
French.   German.   Italian

TWENTY-FOUR TEACHERS EMPLOYED.

Fallows, Rev. Samuel, - - - - 530 Fulton st.
Fallows, Mrs. Rev. Samuel, - - - 530 Fulton st.
Fallows, Eddie - - - - - 530 Fulton st.
Fallows, Miss Helen May, - - - 530 Fulton st.
Filkins, E. A., - - S. E. cor. Centre and Ada.
Filkins, Mrs. E. A., - - S. E. cor. Centre and Ada.
Finlayson, Miss Margaret, - - - 362 S. Wood st.
Foster, Miss Alice, - - - 231 S. Sangamon st.
Fulton, J. L., - - - - - 15 Honore st.
Fulton, Mrs. J. L., - - - - 15 Honore st.

G.

Galloway, A. J., - - - -
Garcelon, M. J., - - - - 233 W. Washington st.
Garcelon, Mrs. M. J., - - - 233 W. Washington st.
Gardner, Mrs., - - - - - 427 Carroll ave.
Gardner, Miss, - - - - 427 Carroll ave.
Garvin, Dr., - - - - - 507 Warren ave.
Garvin, Mrs. Dr., - - - - 507 Warren ave.
Geary, Mrs. A., - - - 681 Van Buren st.
Geary, Miss L., - - - 681 Van Buren st.
Gilbert, Mrs., - - - 681 Van Buren st.
Gilman, Jno., - - - - - 208 W. Lake st.
Gilson, F. G., - - - - -
Goodrich, A., - - - - 335 W. Indiana st.
Goodrich, Mrs. A., - - - - 335 W. Indiana st.
Goodrich, Nellie, - - - - 335 W. Indiana st.
Gould, J. S., - - - - - 180 Sangamon st.
Graham, Wm., - - - - 58 Arbor Place.
Graubert, Mrs., - - - - 639 W. Van Buren st.
Graubert, Miss, - - - 639 W. Van Buren st.
Grey, Mrs., - - - - - 475 Fulton st.
Grey, M. E., - - - - - 11 Park ave.
Grey, Mrs. M. E., - - - - 11 Park ave.
Green, Mrs. A., - - - 302 W. Washington st

Gregg, Miss,	22 Throop st.
Griggs, Jno.,	147 Robey st.
Griggs, Mrs. Jno.,	147 Robey st.
Griggs, Chas. Jr.,	147 Robey st.
Griggs, Mrs.,	302 W. Washington st.
Griggs, Chas. W.,	505 W. Madison st.
Grigor, T. S.,	684 Monroe st.
Grigor, Mrs. T. S.,	684 Monroe st.
Graff, I. N.,	349 Carroll ave.

H.

Hahn, J. H.,	367 Fulton st.
Hahn, Mrs. J. H.,	367 Fulton st.
Hair, W. F.,	52 S. Ann st.
Hair, Mrs. W. F.,	52 S. Ann st.
Hairland, A. C.,	477 Hubbard st.
Hall, E. A.,	47 Warren ave.
Hall, Ernest,	884 Fulton st.
Hall, Mrs. E.,	884 Fulton st.
Hall, O. H.,	222 Madison st.
Harcourt, Wm. L., M. D.,	54 Ann st.
Harcourt, Mrs. Wm. L.,	54 Ann st.
Harcourt, Dr. R. H.,	343 W. Washington st.
Harcourt, John,	343 W. Washington st.
Haworth, P.,	194 E. Jackson st.
Hazard, G. W.,	181 W. Madison st.
Headlam, Wm.,	811 W. Ohio st.
Headlam, Mrs. Wm.,	811 W. Ohio st.
Hecox, W. T.,	525 W. Adams st.
Hecox, Mrs. W. T.,	525 W. Adams st.
Hehnlen, Mrs.,	162 Monroe st.
Hershey, Mrs.,	42 S. Ann st.
Hickox, Mrs. P.,	113 Loomis st.
Hickox, Miss Mabel,	113 Loomis st.

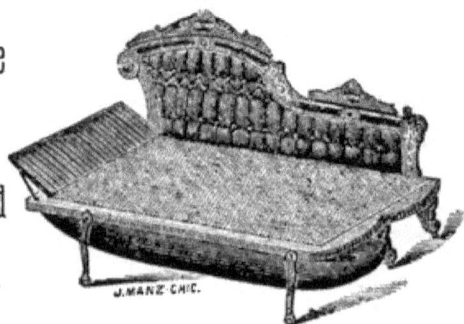

Hill, Miss Nettie, - - - - 290 Warren av.
Hill, R. W. Mrs., - - - 189 N. Carpenter st.
Hill, Albert, - - - - - 189 N. Carpenter st.
Hursell, C. A., - - - - - 364 W. Madison st.
Hursell, J. R., - - - -. 364 W. Madison st.

J.

James, Mrs., - - - - - - 44 St. John's Place.
Jamison, J. N., - - - - - 910 Fulton st.
Jamison, Mrs. J. N., - - - - 910 Fulton st.
Johnson, J. W. - - - - 357 Hubbard st.
Johnson, Mrs. J. W., - - - - 357 Hubbard st.
Johnson, Miss, - - - - 357 Hubbard st.
Johnston Mr., - - - - - 9 Bryan Place.
Johnston, Mrs. - - - - - 9 Bryan Place.
Johnston, Miss C. B., - - - - 9 Bryan Place.
Johnston, A. H. Miss, - - - - 9 Bryan Place.
Johnston, E. P., - - - - 9 Bryan Place.
Jones, F. A. Mrs., - - - - - 49 N. Ann st.
Jones, Mrs., - - - - - Bigsby Place.

K.

Kaycroft, Thos., - - - Cor. Reuben and N. Ann·
Keer, Fred. M., - - - - - 547 Fulton st·
Kennicot, J. W., - - - - 514 Monroe st·
Kidder, Miss A., - Room 10 L. S. and M. S. Depot.
Kimball, E. A., - - - - 44 Loomis st.
Kimball, Mrs. E. W., - - - 44 Loomis st.
King, Lizzie D., - Room 10 L. S. and M. S. Depot.
Knowles, F. P., - - - - 231 Fremont st.
Knowles, F. P., Mrs. - - - - 231 Fremont st.

L.

La Due, J. D., - - - - 393 W. Randolph st.
Landell, John, - - - - 393 W. Randolph st.
Lamb, Wm., - - - - 536 W. Washington st.

Lathrop, A. E., - - - - 74 Walnut st.
Law, Dr. D. H., - - - - 643 W. Madison st.
Lee, Dr., - - - - - 411 W. Jackson st.
Lee, Mrs. Dr., - - - - 411 W. Jackson st.
Leffler, C. C., - - - - 733 W. Madison st.
Lester, T. M., - - - - 342 W. Lake st.
Lester, Dr. J. M., - - - - 342 W. Lake st.
Lewis, W. M., - - - - 95 N. Ada st.
Lewis, Mrs. W. M., - - - - 95 N. Ada st.
Lewis, Brown H., - - - - 75 Ashland ave.
Lord, Miss Ida, - - - - 666 Fulton st.
Lord, J. Sarah, - - - - 666 Fulton st.
Lloyd, Miss, - - - - - 32 Throop st.
Lloyd, Wm., - - - - - 18 Throop st.
Lloyd, R. E., - - - - St. Carolina Court.
Lloyd, J. W., - - - - - 39 Pierce st.
Lloyd, Mrs. J. W., - - - - 39 Pierce st.
Luce, Chas. H., - - - - 702 Monroe st.
Luce, Mrs. Chas. H., - - - - 702 Monroe st.
Luce, Fred., - - - - - 702 Monroe st.

M.

Macauley, Thos., - - - - - 21 N. Halsted st.
Macauley, Mrs., - - - - 21 N. Halsted st.
Macauley, Lizzie, - - - 21 N. Halsted st.
Macomb, Mrs., - - - - 18 S. Ann st.
Magill, Mr., - - - - - 436 W. Jackson st.
Magill, Mrs., - - - - 436 W. Jackson st.
McAllister, H., - - - - 706 Hubbard st.
McAllister, Mrs. H., - - - - 706 Hubbard st.
McDonald, I. H., - - - - 477 S. Oakley st.
McDonald, Mrs., - - - - 542 Lake st.
McHenry, W. E., - - - 456 Washington st.
McIntosh, T. L., - - - - 547 Fulton st.
McIntosh, Mrs. T. L., - - - - 547 Fulton st.

McIntosh, Miss L., - - - - 547 Fulton st.
McIntosh, Miss Fannie, - - - 547 Fulton st.
McIntosh, Miss B., - - - - 547 Fulton st.
J. S. Meckling, - - - 606 W. Washington st.
Miss Meckling, - - 606 W. Washington st.
Merkel, J. P., - - - - - Lake st., near Ann.
Merkel, Mrs. J. P., - - - Lake st., near Ann.
McLean, Mrs., - - - - 15 St. John's place.
Merrill, H. P., - - - - Hyde Park hotel.
Merrill, Mrs. H. P., - - - - Hyde Park hotel.
Merrill, E. M., - - - - Hyde Park hotel.
Merrill, J. P., - - - - - Hyde Park hotel.
Merritt, R., - - - - 59 Warren ave.
Merritt, Mrs. R., - - - - 59 Warren ave.
Mitchell, John, - - - - - 475 Fulton st.
Mitchell, Mrs. John, - - - - 475 Fulton st.
Mochel, J. B., - - - - 342 W. Randolph.
Morgan, Miss, - - - 616 W. Washington st.
Murphy, Wm., - - - - 106 Hermitage ave.
Murphy, Mrs. Wm., - - - 106 Hermitage ave.
Murphy, Miss Grace, - - - 106 Hermitage ave.

N.

Nethercott, Wm., - - - - Austin.
Nethercott, Mrs. Wm., - - - Austin.
Nethercott, Arthur, - - - - Austin.
Noyes, Miss, - - -

O.

Oakes, B. A., - - - 75 Randolph st.
O'Brien, Mrs., - - - 11 Throop st.
O'Donnell, O., - - - 82 N. Sangamon st.
O'Donnell, Mrs. O., - - 82 N. Sangamon st.
Olmstead, J. F., - - - 230 W. Madison st.
Ott, W. C., - - - 567 Fulton st.
Ormsby, Miss L. A., - - 69 N. Sheldon st.

E. W. WESTFALL,

Real Estate Agent

92 WASHINGTON ST.,

(BASEMENT.)

CHICAGO, ILLINOIS.

I still offer my services to *Residents* and *Non-Residents* in *Purchasing, Selling, Leasing*, and taking general care and management of *Real Estate* in Chicago and vicinity.

Loans Negotiated, Rents Collected, and accounts of same promptly rendered.

I do a strictly Agency Businesss, and any matter entrusted to my care will receive prompt and personal attention. I have a *choice* list of *Improved and Unimproved Real Estate* on my books for Sale or Exchange, to which I invite attention personally or by correspondence.

Lots, Blocks, and Acre Property in Hyde Park, South Chicago, and Cornell.

E. W. WESTFALL.

P.

Packard, Theod.,	Sherman House.
Park, Miss Martha,	228 Michigan ave.
Parkhurst, Francis,	384 W. Van Buren st.
Payne, Miss,	167 Walnut st.
Pierce, Mrs.,	
Peloubet, J.,	Cor. Market and Madison sts.
Peloubet, Mrs. J.,	Cor. Market and Madison sts.
Peshall, Capt.,	Bishop Court hotel.
Peshall, Mrs. Capt.,	Bishop Court hotel.
Peterson, L.,	L. S. and M. S. Depot.
Peterson, W.,	479 W. Madison st.
Peterson, Mrs. J.,	
Phillipps, Mrs.,	395 W. Madison st.
Pike, W. E.,	50 S. Ann st.
Pike, Mrs. W. E.,	50 S. Ann st.
Pinto, Miss Lillie,	233 W. Washington st.
Powers, E. F.,	475 W. Randolph st.
Prescott, Mrs. J. C.,	311 W. Monroe st.
Price, Mrs.,	39 Pierce st.
Price, Miss,	39 Pierce st.
Prouty, Chas. B.,	189 N. Carpenter st.
Prouty, Mrs. Chas. B.,	189 N. Carpenter st.
Putman, V. C.,	268 W. Harrison st.
Putman, Mrs. V. C.,	268 W. Harrison st.

Q.

Quilter, Mrs. M. A.,	18 Troop st.

R.

Rainey, G. W.,	53 S. Morgan st.
Rainey, Mrs. G. W.,	53 S. Morgan st.
Rainey, C. J.,	55 S. Morgan st.
Rainey, Mrs. C. J.,	55 S. Morgan st.
Raycroft, J. W.,	504 Noble st.
Reynolds, Mrs.,	459 Washington st.
Reynolds, Dr. B. P.,	115 E. Randolph st.

Richardson, W. H.,	- - -	890 Arnold st.
Rimmer, R. L.,	- -	342 W. Lake st.
Rimmer, Mrs. R. L.,	- -	342 W. Lake st.
Riphan, Mr. M. L.,	- -	97 Park ave.
Rogers, M. L.,	- -	209 Washington st.
Rogers, Mrs. M. L.,	- -	209 Washington st.
Root, W. R.	- - -	
Roach, Mrs.,	- - - -	Barcley block.
Russell, J. T.,	- - -	746 Lake st.
Russell, Mrs. J. T.,	- - - - -	746 Lake st.

S.

Sansum, O. B.,	- -	429 Randolph st.
Sansum, Mrs. O. B.,	- -	429 Randolph st.
Sansum, Miss L.,	- - -	429 Randolph st.
Sansum, Saml..	- - -	429 Randolph st.
Sarassy, Mrs.	- -	364 W. Madison st.
Saunders, Mrs.,	- - -	96 N. Ann st.
Scripture, Mrs. M.	- - -	80 S. Sangamon st.
Scripture, Miss Nellie,	- -	80 S. Sangamon st.
Sellon, Mrs. E. M.,	- - -	22 Throop st.
Sells, W. B.,	- - -	333 Hubbard st.
Sells, Mrs. W. B.,	- - -	333 Hubbard st.
Shaw, Mrs.,	- - -	389 W. Randolph st.
Sherman, Miss,	- - -	316 Indiana st.
Smith, Mrs.,	.. - -	164 Park ave.
Smith, Mrs. Lyman,	- -	638 Lake st.
Smith, Mrs. E. A.,	- - -	963 Lake st.
Smith, James A..	- - -	75 S. Wood st.
Smith, Miss C.,	- - -	16 Centre ave.
St. John, E.,	- .- -	450 Fulton st.
St. John, Mrs. E.,	- - -	450 Fulton st.
Sterritt, Miss Mary,	- -	628 Fulton st.
Sterritt, Miss Lizzie,	- -	628 Fulton st.

F. D. SENIOR AND CO.

DESIGNERS AND ENGRAVERS ON WOOD

CATALOGUE & BOOK ILLUSTRATIONS
PORTRAITS
COLORED WORK &c.

VIEWS OF BUILDINGS INTERIORS
LANDSCAPES MACHINERY &c.

NO. 167
SOUTH CLARK STREET.

BETWEEN
MADISON AND MONROE.

CHICAGO.

Stevens, E. P.,   -   -   338 W. Washington st.
Stevens, Mrs. E. P.,   -   -   338 W. Washington st.
Story, Miss J. A.,   -   -   -   62 Walnut st.
Stryker, Mrs.,   -   -   -   55 S. Peoria st.
Stuart, E. C.,   -   -   -   254 Walnut st.
Stuart, Mrs. E. C.,   -   -   -   254 Walnut st.
Sunnock, G. W.,   -   - ·   ·   15 Will st.
Sweet, W. K.,   -   -   -   600 W. Adams st.
Sweet, Mrs. W. K.,   -   -   600 W. Adams st.

T.

Taylor, Mrs. J. W.,   -   -   -   Maplewood.
Taylor, H. W.,   -   -   -   44 St. John's Place.
Taylor, Mrs. H. W.,   -   -   44 St. John's Place.
Thompson, W. B.,   -   -   162 Park ave.
Thompson, Mrs. W. B.,   -   -   162 Park ave.
Thompson, W. G.,   -   -   133 S. Morgan st.
Thompson, Miss,   -   -   -   133 S. Morgan st.
Thurston, Miss,   -   ·   155 Wilcox ave.
Tiffany, L.,   -   -   231 S. Sangamon st.
Tiffany, D.,   -   -   -   231 S. Sangamon st.
Tiffany, Miss Nellie,   -   231 S. Sangamon st.
Tracey, Wm.,   -   -   343 W. Washington st.
Trent, Edward,   -   -   20 Armor st.
Trent, Mrs. Edward,   -   -   20 Armor st.

U.

Upham, Mrs. E. P.,   -   -   97 Park ave.
Union, U. P.,   -   -   -   504 Noble st.

V.

Valentine, E. R.,   -   -   -   663 Adams st.
Valentine, Mrs. E. R.,   -   -   -   663 Adams st.
Vivian, T.,   -   -   -   16 N. May st.
Vosswinkel, J. P.,   -   -   22 N. Ashland ave.
Vosswinkel, Mrs. J. P.,   -   -   22 N. Ashland ave.
Vosswinkel, F.,   -   -   22 N. Ashland ave.
Vosswinkel, Miss B.,   -   -   22 N. Ashland ave.

W.

Wagner, M. D.,	55 Ashland ave.
Walker, John,	389 Fulton st.
Walker, Mrs. John,	389 Fulton st.
Walker, Miss Annie,	389 Fulton st.
Walker, Albert,	389 Fulton st.
Walker, Wm. A.,	389 Fulton st.
Wallace, Mr.,	44 S. Loomis st.
Wallace, Mrs.,	44 S. Loomis st.
Wainwright, Jas.,	18 Armor st.
Wainwrigbt, Mrs. J.,	18 Armor st.
Webster, P. L.,	70 E. Randolph st.
Westfall, P. R.,	318 W. Monroe st.
Westfall, Mrs. P. R.,	318 W. Monroe st.
Westfall, E. W.,	313 W. Monroe st.
Westfall, Miss Emma,	318 W. Monroe st.
Whitcomb, R. S.,	184 Park ave.
Whitcomb, Mrs. R. S.	184 Park ave.
Whitcomb, Miss S.,	184 Park ave.
Wignall, T. M.,	158 Walnut st.
Willey, Jno. A.,	563 Fulton st.
Williamson, Miss H. E.,	13 Sheldon st.
Willis, W. W.,	16 N. Oakley st.
Willis, Mrs. W. W.,	16 N. Oakley st.
Winter, Mrs.,	159 Park ave.
Winter, N. H.,	368 W. Madison st.
Winter, Mrs. N. H.,	368 W. Madison st.
Wright, A. M.,	701 Jackson st.
Wright, Mrs. A. M.,	701 Jackson st.

Y.

Young, Mr.	71 Park ave

W. B. FARRELL,

FLORIST,

238 WABASH AVE.,

COR. JACKSON STREET.

Plants, Cut Flowers, Bouquets, Baskets, Crosses, Wreaths, Anchors, Hearts, Etc.

V. E. WINCHELL,

Sign & Ornamental

PAINTER,

GRAND PACIFIC HOTEL.

Cor. Jackson and LaSalle Sts.

Send me a Postal to get your Transom numbered,
Price $3.00.

NAMES INADVERTENTLY OMITTED.

A

Adams, Mr. and Mrs. M. C.	64 Throop st
Adams. Master F.	64 Throop st
Agnew, Henry, Sr.,	464 W. Randolph st
Agnew, Henry, Jr.,	26 Arbor place
Agnew, J. L.	464 W. Randolph st
Anderson, Mr. and Mrs. A. F.	327 W. Madison st

B

Ball, Mr. and Mrs. Jas. M.	183 Park av
Balfour, James	316 Hermitage av
Balfour, Mary E.	316 Hermitage av
Beale, Mrs. M.	468 W. Jackson st
Beale, Nellie	468 W. Jackson st
Bigelow, Mrs. Alice E.	841 W. Madison st
Brown, Mr. and Mrs. Ira	13 Park av

C

Craig, Mr. and Mrs. James	35 Park av
Cronkhite, Mr. and Mrs. O.	357 Washington st

D

Dart, Samuel	359 Madison st

G

Grant, Mrs. A. M.	741 Honore st

H

Hopkinson, Miss Lillie	447 Washington st

L

Kleinman, Mr. and Mrs. J. J.	79 Walnut st

M

Meckling, Mrs. J. S.	606 Washington st
McCormack, Mr. and Mrs. S. B.	419 Monroe st

R

Rigley, Mr. and Mrs.	18 Throop st

S

Sheville, Rev. and Mrs. John	125 Dearborn st
Sunnock, Mr. and Mrs. John	15 Will st
Sunnock, Miss M.	15 Will st

T

Towler, Mr. and Mrs. J. P.	122 Honore st

W

Wigley, Fillmore	112 Honore st
Wigley, Misses Nydia and Emma	112 Honore st
Wilcox, Mr. and Mrs. S. N.	440 Washington st

CHANGES OF RESIDENCE.

Ackley, Mr. and Mrs. F. D., and Miss, removed to 293 W. Randolph st
Allen, Mr. and Mrs. John, and Joseph, " to 8 Irving place
Bankson, Mrs. M. . . . " to 231 Fremont st
Carpenter, Miss Emma . . " to 79 Walnut st
Chisholm, Mr. and Mrs. A. E. . " to 14 S. Ashland ave
Colburn, Mr. and Mrs. L. J. . . " to 234 Ontario st
Coles, Miss Jennie . . " to 234 Ontario st
Cox, Mr. and Mrs. W. G., and family " to 297 W. Indiana st
Dart, Mr. and Mrs. Wm. . . " to 344 Monroe st
Dearing, Dr. and Mrs. . . " to Hoyne and Harrison sts
Eckhart, Mr. and Mrs. B. A. . " to 543 Adams st
Fairbanks, Mr. and Mrs. J. . . " to 50 Winchester ave
Johnson, Mr. and Mrs. E. P. . " to 543 Adams st
Johnson, Misses Belle and Ada . . " to 543 Adams st
Rainey, Mr. and Mrs. G. W. . " to 16 Centre av
Rainey, Mr. and Mrs. C. J. . . " to 16 Centre av

Mr. Mayward has removed his Drug Store to the Northeast corner of Lake and Paulina streets, just opposite his old stand. No. 626 W. Lake Street.

Mr. E. W. Westfall will be found at No. 108 Fifth Avenue, basement.

PRESENT CHURCH CHOIR.

Miss Fannie Hancock, *Soprano,* 109 S. Sangamon Street,
Mrs. A. F. Anderson, *Contralto,* 50 S. May Street,
Mr. H. F. Stone, *Tenor,* 356 W. Jackson Street,
Mr. Chas. Lee, *Basso,* 338 W. Washington Street,
W. H. Hodge, *Organist,* 109 S. Sangamon Street.

VESTRY CHANGES.

Messrs. Jas. M. Ball, Wetmore G. Thompson and E. C. Eckhart were elected vestrymen for three years from April 5th, 1876, Messrs. Castle, Raney and Colburn retiring; Mr. John Walker, Treasurer; Mr. E. W. Castle, Parish Secretary.

CORRECTION.

In "Church History," page 33, read Rev. H. N. *Bishop,* instead of Rev. H. N. *Powers.*
Page 51, read Mrs. *E. A.* instead of Mrs. *E. W.* Kimball.

The Young People's Union.

This society was organized October 21st, 1875, and has since steadily increased in numbers and usefulness. Its object is fully set forth in the constitution, following this brief sketch of its history. It has now about fifty members. Since its organization, it has given a series of entertainments of an interesting and instructive character, and the young people intend to keep them up from time to time, and make them still more attractive. They consist chiefly of music, readings, recitations, addresses, debates and the like; the design being to vary the exercises so that all may take a part therein and each find something congenial to his tastes and adapted to his talents. In this way the society will be a source of intellectual and spiritual improvement to the younger members of the congregation, and, if properly conducted, can hardly fail to be productive of much lasting good. Owing to the press of Sabbath-school work, during the Christmas holidays, there have not been as many meetings of the society as could have been wished; but those that have been held give promise of a useful if not a brilliant future. There is certainly material enough in the church to make a first-class society, and under the supervision of the President of the Union, whose experience in such matters has been extensive, it will doubtless be brought into requisition. One thing is certain, the society, collectively and individually, will aim to make welcome those who

WOOD ENGRAVING

In all its different branches executed in the best style of the art, at reasonable prices and on short notice. Particular attention paid to *fine* work, such as Portraits, Landscapes, Buildings, Book Illustrations, Cards, Bill and Letter heads, Monograms, &c.

ROOMS 60 & 61,

29 LaSALLE ST., Corner Washington (Merchants' Building).
TAKE THE ELEVATOR.

J. BERRY,

CONFECTIONER,

Ice Cream, Soda Water,
Caramels,

All kinds of home-made Candies.

Orders for ICE CREAM solicited and delivered.

287 W. Madison Street.

may honor its meetings with their presence. It is, perhaps, too soon to speculate upon its career, as it is yet merely in its infancy; but it is *not* too much to bespeak for it an earnest, unfaltering support from the members of the church and congregation. This I do, knowing well that it has at heart the social and moral well-being of the youth upon whom the future prosperity and stability of the church will very largely depend. I ask also a careful perusal of the subjoined constitution.

Constitution of the "Young People's Union."

Article I.—The name of this organization shall be "The Young People's Union," of St. Paul's Reformed Episcopal Church.

Article II.—Its object shall be religious, literary and social culture.

Article III.—Its officers shall be a president, vice-president, secretary and treasurer, and an executive committee consisting of (5) five persons, which officers shall be elected by ballot at each semi-annual meeting of the Union, to be held on the first Tuesday evenings of November and May, and shall take their seats on the evening of their election and serve until their successors shall be elected and placed in office.

Article IV.—There shall be four sub-committees appointed by the executive committee at the meeting immediately following the annual meeting, to be known as the stranger's committee, the devotional committee, the membership committee, and the publishing committee, and shall perform their duties respectively for six months or until their successors shall be elected.

Article V.—A committee of one (1) lady and two (2) gentlemen shall be appointed by the executive committee at each regular meeting, to be known as the Entertainment Committee, whose duty it

shall be to prepare and carry into execution a programme of exercises for the next succeeding meeting.

Article VI.—It shall be the duty of the president to preside at all meetings in accordance with parliamentary usages, of the vice-president to preside in the absence of the president, of the secretary to keep all records of the Union, do all corresponding for the Union, and at the expiration of his term of office to turn over to his successor all books and papers in his possession, of the treasurer to collect all fees and assessments from members, to take charge of all moneys belonging to the Union subject to its order, and at the expiration of his or her term of office to make a full report of the financial condition of the Union, and to turn over to his or her successor all moneys in his or her possession.

Article VII.—The executive committee shall consist of president, vice-president, secretary and two (2) members of the Union, to be elected at the semi-annual meeting. Its duties shall be to appoint the sub-committees, issue calls for special meetings, decide on place for holding the meetings, and take charge under the instruction of the Union, of all matters not herein provided for.

Article VIII.—The devotional committee shall consist of three (3) persons, one (1) lady and two (2) gentlemen, and they shall have in charge all devotional meetings of the Union, appointing leaders for same and doing all in their power to advance the spiritual interests of the Union.

Article IX.—The stranger's committee shall consist of five (5) members, two (2) ladies and three (3) gentlemen, whose duty it shall be to cultivate the acquaintance of strangers attending church services, and to introduce them to its individual members. To accomplish this, at least two members of the committee shall be in attendance at the regular service fifteen (15) minutes before and after service.

Article X.—The membership committee shall consist of five (5) persons, two (2) ladies and three (3) gentlemen, whose duty it shall be to consider the qualification of applicants for membership, recommending to the Union only'such as they know to be of good moral character, which recommendation must be concurred in by at least three members of the committee and approved by a two-thirds vote of the members present, after which they shall be introduced to the Union by the president, pay their initiation fee, sign the constitution and be declared members.

Article XI.—The publishing committee shall consist of three (3) persons, one (1) lady and two (2) gentlemen, and it shall be their duty to print or publish any paper, pamphlet, programme, notice or other matter which the Union may direct to be printed or published.

Article XII.—The initiation fee shall be fifty cents (50 c.). There shall also be a semi-annual tax of twenty-five cents (25c.) for each member, and a fine of ten cents (10c.) for non-attendance at its meetings for each failure to attend.

Article XIII.—The regular meeting of the Union shall be held on the first and third Tuesday evenings of each month in the church parlors or elsewhere.

Article XIV.—Any person receiving a four-fifth's majority vote for expulsion shall cease to be a member.

Article XV.—Order of exercises: Promptly at 8 o'clock the members shall be called to order by the proper officers and the meeting shall be opened by prayer. The minutes of the last meeting shall be read, new members shall be received and any new business taken up. The literary and musical programmes shall then be proceeded with, after which any innocent form of amusement will be in order.

Article XVI.—Nine members shall constitute a quorum, and a majority vote shall have all the force of a unanimous vote, when not otherwise specified by the constitution.

Article XVII.—This constitution may be amended at any time by a two-thirds vote of all the members present, notice having been given of proposed amendments in writing at a meeting which shall have occurred at least one week previous.

Officers and Members of Young People's Union.

E. C. ECKHARDT, President.
MISS LUA CUMMINGS, Vice-President,
E. P. STEVENS, Secretary.
FRED. M. KERR, Treasurer.

W. M. LEWIS,
JOHN HARCOURT,
MRS. FAIRBANKS. } Strangers' Committee.
MRS. ST. JOHN,
MISS SANSUM,

MISS M. GRACE BRYAN,
MISS SUSIE WHITCOMB, } Entertainment Committee
and Executive Committee.

Adams, Miss Carrie,
Bennett, Mr. J. W.
Bishop, Mr. F. H.
Brannan, Miss Bessie M.
Brooks, Mr. E. P.
Brown, Mr. Ira.
Brown, Mrs. Ira.
Bryan, Mr. Wm. A.
Bryan, Mr. H. A.
Bryan, Mr. A. C.
Colburn, Mr. L. J.
Colburn, Mrs. L. J.
Cummings, Miss Lua,
Durand, Mr. Elliot,
Eckhart, Mr. B. A.
Hall, Mr. Olin H.
Hazard, G. W.
Hill, Miss Nettie,
Hill, Mr. H. D.
Kerr, Mr. Frederick M.
Landell, Mr. John E.
Lewis, Mrs. W. M.
McIntosh, Miss Fannie,
McIntosh, Miss Lavinia,
McIntosh, Mr. J. H.
Mills, Chas.
Olmstead, Mr. J. F.
Powers, Mr. Ed. F.
Reynolds, Dr. B. P.
St. John, Mr. A. E.
Sansum, Mr. O. B.
Thompson, Mr. W. B.
Thompson, Mrs. W. B.
Tracy, Wm.
Van Michalouske, Mr. T.
Whitcomb, R. S.

SHEPHERD,

FLORAL

ARTIST,

99 STATE ST.,

AT

HAMILTON, ROWE & CO.'S

JEWELRY STORE.

Floral Work of every description cheap. Plants in season for house or garden.

D. W. Van Cott and Co.,

JEWELERS

AND

Watchmakers,

224 State St., cor. Quincy,

Is the Cheapest place in the city to buy Watches, Chains, Jewelry and Silverware.

Repairing and Engraving a Specialty.

The Woman's Association

OF THE

ST. PAUL'S R. E. CHURCH.

The first meeting of the Woman's Society of this Church was held in the church parlors on May 11th, 1875, and a Constitution and By-Laws submitted and approved. They have continued to hold meetings every fortnight since that time, either at the church or at the house of some member of the organization. A perusal of the Constitution will satisfy those interested that the management of it is in good hands, and that the ladies mean business. They also have given a series of entertainments during the present season, which have always been well attended, and have been interesting throughout. They have done much toward promoting the sociability of the church members, and in their work of charity have made glad the hearts of many a deserving family, and kept from want some who would otherwise have been destitute. The ladies should be congratulated upon their good fortune in securing a President who is so well posted in church management generally, so capable in every way of filling the position to which she has been elected.

A Ladies' Missionary Society is also to be organized from which we confidently look for good results.

CONSTITUTION AND BY-LAWS.

NAME AND OBJECT.

Article I.—The name of the Association shall be called the Woman's Association of "St. P. R. E. Church"—its object to co-operate for the spiritual and temporal advancement of St. Paul's Church.

OFFICERS AND THEIR POWERS.

Article II.—The officers shall consist of a President, Vice-President, Secretary, and Treasurer, and nine managers, all of whom shall constitute a "Board of Managers," a majority of whom shall constitute a quorum for the transaction of business, and the general business and management of the Association shall be vested in this Board.

DUTY OF OFFICERS.

Article III.—It shall be the duty of the President to preside at all meetings of the Association and "Board of Managers," and to be the general executive officer of the same. It shall be the duty of the Vice-President to fill her place in her absence or inability. It shall be the duty of the Secretary to keep a record of all proceedings, to call the roll, to read the minutes and to notify the Treasurer in meeting of any indebtedness to the Association. It shall be the duty of the Treasurer to take charge of all moneys, collect all fines, keeping an account of the same, and to disburse only upon order of the Secretary countersigned by the President.

MEETINGS.

Article IV.—The annual meeting shall be held the Wednesday following the annual parish meeting, when all officers shall be elected—old officers serving until their successors are duly elected and have qualified. The Association and Board of Managers to meet every other Friday unless otherwise ordered by the President, who may call at any time a special meeting.

VACANCIES.

Article V.—All vacancies by death or illness or inability shall be temporarily filled by some member of the Board of Managers to be selected by the president until the first regular meeting thereafter, when the place shall be filled after the manner of ordinary election.

CHANGES.

Article VI.—Changes may be made in the constitution or by-laws by a concurrent vote of the majority of the association and Board of Managers, all such changes being first preferred to and approved by the Board of Managers, and shall be submitted to the approval of the association at least two weeks before a vote is taken.　　·

BY-LAWS.

MEMBERSHIP.

Article I.—Any woman may upon recommendation by a member of the association become a member of the same by a two-thirds vote of the Board of Managers and payment of an initiation fee of 50c.

REMOVAL.

Article II.—The Board of Managers shall have power to remove or suspend any member or officer of the association by a two-thirds vote of the Board of Managers, subject to an appeal to the association.

BUREAUS AND COMMITTEES.

Article III.—The Board of Managers shall have power to form such bureaus and committees as shall seem necessary to accomplish the purposes of the organization; to determine the character of committees as standing or special; to select the head or chairman of each; to make such rules and regulations to govern the same as shall be necessary; to determine the number constituting each committee, drawing the same in alphabetical order from the association.

PENALTIES AND ABSENTMENTS.

Article IV.—Three consecutive absentments without leave of absence from the secretary or treasurer shall subject any officer to a fine of not less than 25c., and five absentments, illness excepted, will remove from office. Each absentment of a member of the association will be subject to a fine of five cents. A refusal to serve in alphabetical order upon any committee, heads of bureaus and chairmen excepted, will subject each person to a fine of not less than 25c.

Article V.—All committees shall be subject to the control of the Board of Managers.

RECORDS AND REPORTS.

Article VI.—All records of the association shall be open to inspection at any public meeting, and all reports of bureaus and committees shall be in meeting.

MONEYS.

Article VII.—No moneys can be expended without the consent of a majority of the Board of Managers.

Ladies' Association.

OFFICERS AND MEMBERS.

BOARD OF MANAGERS.

Mrs. WRIGHT, President.
" LEWIS, Vice-President.
" RANEY, Secretary.
" ST. JOHN, Treasurer.
" Adams,
" Chisholm,
" Fallows,
" Russell,
" Taylor,
" Hull,
" Walker,
" Colburn,
" Whitcomb.

Mrs. Arnold,
" Ackley,
" Allen,
" Beal,
" Carpenter,
Miss Carpenter,
Mrs. Geary,
" Hull,
" Hickcox,
" Johnson,

Mrs. Merritt,
" McGill,
" Prescott,
" Peterson,
" G. W. Raney,
" Stuart,
" Smith,
" Voswinkle,
" Valentine,
" Walkley.

The Sabbath School,

A Sabbath School with an average attendance of over two hundred scholars, with a zealous and efficient staff of teacher, and a wise superintendency over all its interests, will be more than likely to succeed; and such is the condition of our Sabbath School after an existence of but seven months; and inasmuch as its past prosperity has exceeded even the most sanguine anticipations of those interested, why not expect as much in the future? The Superintendent has been ever alive to the responsibility of his office, striving always to increase the membership by enticing to our school, only those, however, who were halting in their choice, and who were not members of any other school.

The interesting and practical explanations of the lessons each Sunday, either by him or Dr. Fallows, could not fail to arouse a desire in the most careless and indifferent scholar to learn more of the blessed truths taught in Sabbath School.

The Bible Class also, under the management of Prof. Church, is each Sunday not only becoming larger, but

the sixty members seem keenly alive to the advantages
afforded by thus meeting together weekly, perusing carefully that priceless gift to man, the Bible. And while the
Superintendent, Assistant Superintendent, and Teachers
have been engaged in their good work, the Library has
not been neglected; and Messrs. Whitcomb and St. John
deserve especial credit for the judicious management they
have displayed in this all-important branch of the Sabbath School.

Sunday School Officers.

President *ex officio:* DR. FALLOWS.
Superintendent: COL. BENNETT.
Assistant-Superintendent: L. J. COLBURN.
Librarian: R. S. WHITCOMB.
First Assistant Librarian: E. St. JOHN.
Second "   "   E. W. WESTFALL.
Treasurer: JOHN WALKER.
Secretary: JOHN HARCOURT.
Assistant Secretary: HENRY BRYAN.
Musical Instructor: H. P. MERRILL.
Pianist: MRS. ST. JOHN.

Sunday School Teachers.

BIBLE CLASS No. 1, Prof. M. D. Church.
" " No. 2, Mr. P. R. Westfall.
" " No. 3, Mr. John Walker.
" " No. 4, Miss Cora Benson.
" " No. 5, Miss Bertha Benson.
" " No. 6, Miss Ada Benson.
" " No. 7, Miss E. Clow.
" " No. 8, Mr. Wainwright.
" " No. 9, Mrs. St. John.
" " No. 10, Mrs. Lewis.
" " No. 11, Miss Whitcomb.
" " No. 12, Mr. Mills.
" " No. 13, { Mrs. Hull. / Miss Ina L. Ackley.
" " No. 14, Mr. G. W. Hazard.
" " No. 15, Mr. J. Fairbanks.

BIBLE CLASS.

MR. M. D. CHURCH, Teacher.

Allen, Mrs. John.......................245½ Walnut st.
Armstrong, Miss K....................401 W. Jackson st.

Bryan, Miss M. Grace...................1 Bryan Place.

Beach, Miss H. W... ....457 W. Jackson st.

Carpenter, Miss Maria...............21 St. John's Place.
Chisholm. Mrs. H......................9 Irving Place.
Clark, Miss Belle.........................71 Park ave.
Clark, Miss Mary.......................71 Park ave.
Clarkson, Miss.............................
Clydesdale, Miss............Washington and Desplaines.
Cooper, Miss Nettie........................19 S. Ann st.
Colburn, Mrs. Levi J......................71 Park ave.
Cox, Miss M. A., ⎫
Cox, Miss L. A., ⎬ ....352 Ohio st.
Cox, Mr. W. G., ⎭
Coyne, Miss M. E.....................216 Ogden ave.
Crane, Mr. E...............307 W. Washington st.
Crane, Mr. C. R.................369 W. Washington st.
Cummings, Miss Eva.........St. Caroline's Court Hotel.

Dorenberg, Miss M...............42 Union Park Place.

Fairbanks, Mr. John....................710 Monroe st.
Fairbanks, Mrs. John....................710 Monroe st.
Fallows, Mrs. Sam'l.......................530 Fulton st.
Fretz, Mr................................

Gilson, Miss F. G...................318 W. Harrison st.
Gray, Mrs...............................475 Fulton st

Hall, O. H........................346 W. Madison st.
Harcourt, Mrs. W. L......................54 S. Ann st.
Haworth, Mr. P....................194 E. Jackson st.
Hazard, Mr. G. W....................78 Van Buren st.
Hickox, Mabel.........................113 Leavitt st.
Holway, Mr. A.....................52 S. Ann st.

Johnson, Miss........................9 Bryan Place.

Johnson, Miss Belle....................9 Bryan Place.

King, Miss Lizzie........Room 10 L. S. and M. S. Depot.

La Due, Mr. J. D..................393 W. Randolph st.
Landell, Mr. John..................393 W. Randolph st.
Laster, Mr. Thos. M....................342 W. Lake st.
Lathrop, N. H...........................74 Walnut st.
Lewis, Mr. M. W.......................69 Sheldon st.
Lloyd, A. E.......................St. Caroline's Court.

McCauley, Mr. Thos....................21 N. Halsted st.
McCauley, Miss Lizzie.................21 N. Halsted st.
McIntosh, Miss L......................547 Fulton st.
McIntosh, Miss Fannie..................547 Fulton st.

Pinto, Miss Lulu................233 W. Washington st.
Peterson, Miss F................L. S. and M. S. Depot.

Sansum, Miss Lulu................429 W. Randolph st.
Scripture, Miss Nellie...............80 S. Sangamon st.
Sherman, Miss H. M....................316 Indiana st.
Steritt, Miss Lizzie.......................628 Fulton st.
Steritt, Miss Mary.......................628 Fulton st.
Story, Miss............................62 Walnut st.
Stuart, C. E...........................254 Walnut st.
Sunnock, Mr. S. W.......................15 Will st.

Tiffany, Mr. N. G............Sangamon st., near Halsted.
Treacy, Mr. Wm.................343 W. Washington st.

Wright, Mrs. A. M...................701 W. Jackson st.

Scholars of St. Paul's Sunday School.

A.

Adams, Mabel
Allen, John
Ames, Edith

Armstrong, K.
Ayres, Lulu
Armstrong, A.

B.

Benson, R.
Benson, Nellie
Benson, Chas.
Boyle, Alex.

Bryan, A. B.
Bryan, C. M.
Bryan, Chas.
Boyle, W.

C.

Carpenter, Arthur
Carpenter, Chas.
Carpenter, May,
Carrelton, Kittie
Castello, Emma
Chase, Herbert
Clark, I.
Clydardale, Ida
Coles, Jennie
Coles, Alice
Conners, Ed.
Cook, Alice
Cox, Fred

Cox, Ella
Cox, Augusta
Coyne, Minnie
Crane, Ada
Cooper, Nettie
Carpenter, E.
Cummings, L. W.
Carpenter, H.
Clydersdale, Mary
Clydersdale, John
Cludas, Ida
Cludas, Chas..

D.

Dayton, Fannie
Dayton, Jessie

Demples, Cornelius
Demples, Susan

Houses for sale or rent at North Evanston by JOHN CULVER, *S.
W. Cor. Clark and Washington Sts.*

Demples, Al.

Driscol, Maggie

F.

Fallows, E. F.

Foster, Geo.

Fallows, Mary

Foster, Alice

Fallows, Alice

Fostey, May

Flaherty, Pat

Fulton, Thos.

Flaherty, Mary

Francis, Parkhurst

Flaherty, Annie

Francis, Lulu

G.

Geary, L.

Granbert, Nettie

Goodrich, Nellie

Gray, Willie

Groff, Ella S.

Gray, Grace

Groff, Etta

H.

Hall, Katie

Helman, Geo.

Harcourt, Nellie M.

Herron, Lester

Harmon, Annie

Hill, Alice

Harmount, P.

Holin, Harry

Haines, Bessie

Hook, John

Haines, Herbert

Hook, Fred

Haines, Fred

Holliday, Milton

Hartman, Augusta

Herron, Prisley

Hartman, Donnie

Hickcox, Mabel

Hartman, Mary

Hill, Fred

Hayden, F.

J.

Johnson, A.

Jamison, James

Johnson, Ella

K.

Kidder, A.

Klyneman, John

Kittenger, L.
Klyneman, Wm.

Klyneman, Oliver
Kraefft, Harry

L.

Larson, Chas.
Larson, Mary
Larson, Emma
Lewis, Brown

Little, Eddie
Lord, Eva
Lyke, Carrie
Lyke, Lottie

M.

McCormick, Fannie
McCowley, Geo.
McCowley, E.
McCowley, Susan
McDonald, Lennie
McDonald, Louis
McGill, Alice
McIntosh, Minnie
Merritt, Henry

Merritt, Fanny
Merritt, Helen
Merritt, Sarah
Monser, Geo.
Morris, Mary
Morris, Eva
Morse, Arthur
Murphy, Austin
Murphy, Wm.

N.

Nelson, Geo.
Nelson, John

Nye, Frank

O.

O'Donald, Herbert

Oleson, Carry

P.

Page, Chas.
Page, Ed.
Page, John
Pearsons, Geo.

Philipps, L.
Philipps, Lottie
Philipps, Chas.

R.

Randolph, Wm.

Ross, Unity

Reynolds, Alma
Ross, Annie

Rowley, Harry

S.

Sanford, Thomas
Saunders, Lottie,
Saunders, Wm.
Saunders, Mary
Sansum, Mary
Sansum, Jessie
Sarasay, Eva
Sarsis, Robie
Switzer, Eddie
Shaw, Arthur
Simons, Wm.
Sleight, Isabella
Sleight, Annie
Sleight, J.
Slyder, Willie

Smith, Carrie
Smith, J.
Smith, Metha
Smith, C.
Spate, Wm.
Stuart, Bertie
Stuart, Frank
Sweet, Eva
Sleight, John
Sinclair, Eva
Sykes,
Stevens, E. P.
Stevens, Mrs. E. P.
Stevens, Master

T.

Terrill, John
Thompson, Fannie

Trent, Geo.

V.

Vivian, Jenny
Vosswinkel, B.

Vosswinkel. Carrie
Vosswinkel, Fred

W.

Walk, Fred
Walker, Minnie
Walker, Emma
Walker, Albert
Walker, Annie
Wainswright, Sarah

Westfall, Maggie
Westfall, E.
White, Geo.
Winter, Geo.
Wood, Hattie
Wrath, Willie

No. 379 WEST MADISON ST.,
COR. OF ANN.

Wm. Ahlborn's
ART STUDIO.

Old Pictures of all kinds Copied and Enlarged
to any size, and Finished in Oil, India Ink,
Water Colors, Crayon, Pastel, etc., etc.,
in the Most Approved Styles of
the Art.

No. 379 WEST MADISON ST.,
COR. OF ANN.

Wainswright, E.
Waugh, Sophie
Waugh, Pollie

Wright, Charlie
Wright, Hallie
Wilson, Kittie

Y.

Young, Josie
Young, Mamie

Young, Alma

By Laws of the St. Paul's Reformed Episcopal Church of the City of Chicago.

ARTICLE I.

This Parish shall be designated and known as the ST. PAUL'S REFORMED EPISCOPAL CHURCH of the City of Chicago.

ARTICLE II.

The St. Paul's Reformed Episcopal Church of the City of Chicago hereby accedes to, accepts and pledges conformity to the Constitution, Canons and Faith of the Reformed Episcopal Church of America.

ARTICLE III.

SECTION 1.—The officers of this church shall consist

of a Senior Warden, a Junior Warden, and nine Vestrymen. The Senior and Junior Wardens shall be selected annually and hold their respective offices for the period of one year, and until their successors are duly elected and qualified. Three Vestrymen shall be elected annually, whose term of service shall be for the period of three years, and until their successors are duly elected and qualified. The present Wardens and Vestry, elected on the 5th of April, 1875, shall serve for the terms for which they were respectively elected, and until their successors are duly elected and qualified.

SEC. 2.—Any vacancy which may from any cause exist or occur in any of the foregoing offices may be filled by the Wardens and Vestry.

SEC. 3.—All elections by the congregation shall be by ballot and a majority of all the ballots cast shall be necessary for a choice.

SEC. 4.—In case of a failure from any cause to accomplish an annual election, as hereinbefore provided, said election shall be appointed for every succeeding Monday thereafter, in course, until accomplished, as hereinbefore provided.

ARTICLE IV.

The Wardens and Vestry shall constitute a Board for the transaction of the temporal business of the parish, a majority of whom shall constitute a quorum.

They shall appoint a Secretary and Treasurer and such other subordinate officers, agents and employes as they may deem necessary for the purposes of the parish. They shall also have power to provide a Rector for the parish, and such other clerical assistance as he may require, and to adopt such measures for their support and for carrying on the other work of the church, as they shall deem proper and expedient. They shall also have power to appoint all representatives to which this parish shall be entitled in any legislative or judicial body in the Reformed Episcopal Church of America, not otherwise provided for by the canons of the same.

ARTICLE V.

It shall be the duty of the Senior Warden to preside at all meetings of the Wardens and Vestry, and to perform such other duties as are prescribed by the canons of the Reformed Episcopal Church. It shall be the duty of the Junior Warden to perform all the duties of the Senior Warden in case of his absence or disability, and generally to co-operate with and assist the Senior Warden in the discharge of his duties.

ARTICLE VI.

It shall be the duty of the Secretary, upon the request of the Rector or Senior Warden, or upon the written request of any three members of the Board, to call meetings of the Wardens and Vestry for such special purposes as may be set forth in the written notice of the Secretary, which may be served personally or by messenger upon the Wardens and Vestrymen. Such notice shall be deemed sufficient when mailed to the business or residence address of any Warden or Vestryman. He shall keep a record of the proceedings of the Board; shall take charge of all papers and documents of the parish, and perform such other duties as usually pertain to the office of a Secretary or Clerk.

ARTICLE VII.

It shall be the duty of the Treasurer to collect all parish revenues and to receive and care for all its property and effects. He shall disburse the funds of the parish as ordered by the Wardens and Vestry, and shall preserve proper vouchers for all such disbursements. He shall keep a detailed and accurate account of all receipts and expenditures in books to be provided by the parish, which books shall be carefully preserved and at all times be open for the examination of the Board. He shall make an annual statement to the parish of all receipts and disbursements during the last parish year, and shall also make a full exhibit of the financial condition of the parish at the close of the year. He shall also perform such other duties pertaining to his office as the Board may from time to time require.

ARTICLE VIII.

No appropriation of money or other property of the

parish exceeding in value the sum of fifty dollars shall be made by the Wardens and Vestry except upon a motion offered and duly seconded at a regular meeting of the Board, at least one month prior to a vote being taken thereupon.

ARTICLE IX.

The Senior Warden shall appoint annually, subject to the approval of the Board, the following Standing Committees:

A COMMITTEE ON FINANCE, to consist of three members of the Board;

A COMMITTEE ON CHURCH BUILDING, to consist of three members of the Board;

A COMMITTEE ON MUSIC, to consist of three members of the Board or of the congregation;

A COMMITTEE ON PARISH WORK, to consist of three members of the Board, three male members of the congregation, and six female members of the congregation.

ARTICLE X.

All persons of legal age who shall contributed to the support of the parish, and who shall have been *bona fide* members of the congregation for the period of three months next preceding, shall be deemed qualified voters in this parish.

ARTICLE XI.

The Wardens and Vestry shall hold regular or stated

meetings on the first Monday following the first Sunday in every month. Such regular or stated meetings may be adjourned from time to time to any date preceding the next regular or stated meeting; and any such adjourned meeting shall have full power to transact any business which may be transacted by a regular stated meeting of such Wardens and Vestry.

ARTICLE XII.

Special meetings of the Wardens and Vestry may be called by the Rector or Senior Warden, by public notice announced at any regular religious service of the Church.

ARTICLE XIII.

The customary and established Parliamentary Rules of Order and proceedings shall prevail at all meetings of the congregation and of the Wardens and Vestry.

ARTICLE XIV.

Changes in these By-Laws may be made by a vote of two-thirds of the congregation present at a special or annual parish meeting. *Provided:* No such change shall be made until the proposed change shall have been first approved by a vote of at least two-thirds of the Wardens and Vestry at a regular meeting of the same.

Adopted at the parish meeting held Monday evening, April 19, 1875.

Attest,   E. St. John,
                                                            Secretary.

I have thought it advisable to append an extract from the *Chicago Times* concerning the church. Its perusal is recommended, notwithstanding the fact, that some of the items therein contained appear elsewhere in this church history.

(*Extract from the Chicago Sunday Times, Feb. 13th, 1876.*)

HISTORICAL SKETCH OF

St. Paul's Reformed Episcopal.

However unwelcome the fact may be to the friends of the Episcopal church, there is no denying that what is known as the "Reformed Episcopal church" is making rapid headway in Chicago, and has already done the mother church a serious, if not permanent, injury. When Bishop Cheney walked off with his entire congregation, it was remarked by churchmen that the event had no significance, since it was an every-day occurrence to see preachers carry their congregations bodily into some other denomination. "The test will be when these schismatics shall make the attempt to start a new church," said they; "then you will see them break down."

The logic of this prediction was generally admitted, and there were few, even among those who held a friendly attitude toward the "secessionists," who believed they could do much in the way of organizing new churches, the rather as the ground, especially in Chicago, on the part of Episcopalianism *per se*, was already remarkably well covered—in fact, covered more thickly than was consistent with financial prosperity.

Yet, what is it that Episcopalians see to-day? They see on the West side a Reformed Episcopal Church, begun without an organized nucleus, grown within a year to dimensions that eclipse any regular Episcopal church in the same region.

The growth of St. Paul's Reformed Episcopal Church is one of the most remarkable events in the history of Chicago churches. It is probably not too much to say that its increase has been greater than that of any other like organization within the limits of the city, and this in the face of the fact that regular Episcopal churches all about it are quite well satisfied if they hold their own.

Much of the prosperity of St. Paul's can be accounted for on grounds other than mere love for reformed Episcopalianism and dissatisfaction with the mother church. The location of the new organization is excellent, being in the very heart of the well-to-do portion of the West side; the minister is one of the most popular in the city, and exercises a strong personal influence; the congregation is imbued with the enthusiasm that is ever found belonging to new enterprises, and especially when its adherents believe themselves "persecuted," and hence there is a liveliness about all the matters connected with the church that is peculiarly attractive.

It is just about a year ago that Bishop Cheney conceived the idea of forming a permanent organization in the populous West division, and with that view, alternating with his assistant rector, Mr. Postlethwaite, held three Sunday afternoon services in the American Reformed Church, on West Washington, near Ann street. But the weather being extremely cold, owing to a defect in the heating apparatus it was found impossible to keep the edifice properly warmed. Accordingly old St. John's Church, on St. John's Place, opposite Union park, was engaged for future services, which were thereafter, as before, held but once a week.

This arrangement was continued till Easter, when a permanent organization was effected. On the second Monday after Easter St.

Paul's Reformed Episcopal Church was organized with between forty and fifty families, and the following officers were chosen:

Senior Warden—A. M. Wright.

Junior Warden—Col. J. W. Bennett.

Vestrymen—F. A. Bryan, John Walker, R. S. Whitcomb, Devotion Eddy, J. P. Merrill, E. St. John, C. W. Castle, L. J. Colburn, G. W. Raney.

The organization perfected, the church extended a call to Rev. Samuel Fallows, D. D., to become its pastor. The doctor at this time was president of the Wesleyan university of the Methodist Central Conference at Bloomington. After holding the call under advisement for a month, an acceptance was forwarded, and on the first of last July the new pastor entered upon a ministry that cannot be regarded other than one of the most successful in the church history of Chicago.

That Dr. Fallows is a "worker," may be inferred from his history. When the war of the rebellion broke out he left a high position in connection with the University of Appleton to accept a chaplaincy in the army. Subsequently he raised a regiment and fought his way to a generalship. After the war he preached to the Methodists of Milwaukee for three years, and was by them regarded as the most effective minister that had ever settled in their midst. He was next elected state superintendent of instruction of Wisconsin, was a regent of the University, and finally was chosen president of the Wesleyan University at Bloomington, from which position he was taken to fill the pulpit of St. Paul's. In the language of one of his parishioners, Dr. Fallows is a man "who keeps." He is a fluent and impressive speaker, a genial companion, and to a mind of the broadest culture he adds a large capacity for sterling work.

When the vestry extended their call to Dr. Fallows the congregation still worshiped in the old rookery on St. John's Place; but with his advent, the handsome American Reformed Church on Washington street was again engaged for services, and there they have been continued since. What the parish will do for a permanent place of

worship, remains to be decided. But what they are determined not
to do, is to run head over ears in debt, as other churches have done
to their utter ruin and annihilation. The edifice now occupied by
them is advertised for sale; but the St. Paul people feel assured
that whoever may buy the property will be only too glad to retain
them as tenants, and by and by, when they can afford it, they may
decide to take the property off the owner's hands. Certainly the site
cannot be much improved upon.

The church, as has been said, organized one year ago with between 40 and 50 families; when Dr. Fallows became rector it numbered about 70; now, after less than eight months of labor, the ag-
gregate has swelled to 189 families, while of communicants there
are about 200. The general attendance is excellent, and the pew rent
fully covers the running expenses of the church, and while much
has had to be bought, the church is practically out of debt.

In connection with the church is a Sunday-school with an average attendance of about 250 scholars, supplied with a library of 300
volumes, the purchase fund for which was largely raised by the
Young People's Union, a most vivacious organization, addicted to
the giving of very enjoyable entertainments. There is also a vig-
orous Ladies' Society connected with the church, whose works of
charity have called down on the devoted heads of its members many
blessings from the poor of the parish.

Finally, it must be mentioned that the church is provided with
an excellent choir, composed of C. C. Lefler, basso and leader; C. F.
Saxton, tenor, Miss Jessie Hardy, soprano, and Mrs. M. M. Dutton,
alto. The concerts under the auspices of the church, arranged during
the present winter by Mr. Lefler, are generally regarded among the
most attractive ever given in Chicago in connection with a church.

The membership has been largely recruited from the surrounding
and established Episcopal parishes, but a considerable percentage
is due accessions from most other evangelical denominations.

INDEX OF CHURCH DIRECTORY.

PAGE.

Organization of Reformed Episcopal Church ..... 7 to 29
St. Paul's Church History .... 31 to 37
Directory of Church Congregation .... 39 to 63
Young People's Union........................ 65 to 71
The Woman's Association .... 73 to 78
The Sabbath School .... 79 to 89
By-Laws of St. Paul's Reformed Episcopal Church 89 to 94
Extract from Chicago *Times* .... 95 to 98